BRAIN GAMES®

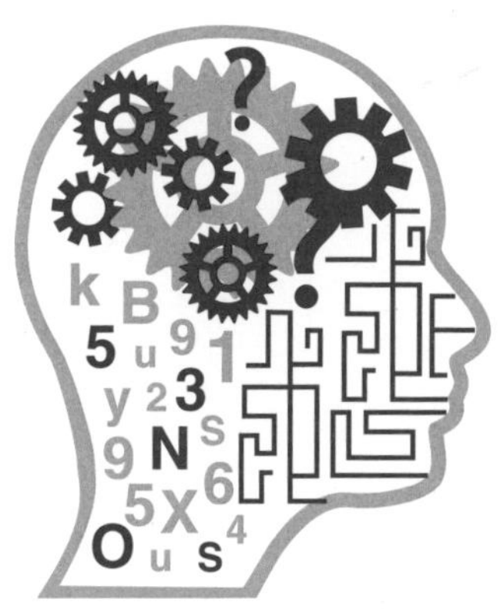

pil

Publications International, Ltd

Contributing Writer: Holli Fort

Puzzlers: Michael Adams, Cihan Altay, Myles Callum, Kelly Clark, Jeanette Dall, Mark Danna, Harvey Estes, Josie Faulkner, Serhiy Grabarchuk, Dick Hess, Marilynn Huret, Nicole H. Lee, David Millar, Alan Olschwang, Ellen F. Pill, Ph.D., Paul Seaburn, Fraser Simpson, Terry Stickels, Howard Tomlinson

Additional Puzzle Editing: Fraser Simpson

Illustrators: Nicole H. Lee, Anna Lender, Bill Perry, Dave Roberts, Marilyn Roberts, Shavan R. Spears

Back Cover Puzzles: Josie Faulkner, David Millar, Shavan R. Spears

Louis Weber, CEO
Publications International, Ltd.
8140 Lehigh Avenue
Morton Grove, Illinois 60053

ISBN-13: 978-1-4127-1453-2
ISBN-10: 1-4127-1453-2

Manufactured in China.

8 7 6 5 4 3 2 1

CONTENTS

BRAIN FITNESS

Your mind is your most important asset—more important than your house, your bank account, or your stock portfolio. You insure your house and work hard to pad your bank account. But what can you do to sharpen your mind and protect it from decline? With the baby boomers getting on in years, an increasing number of people are asking this question. Modern-day science provides a clear answer: You can safeguard your mind by protecting your brain. To understand this relationship further, we turn to cutting-edge research.

Protect and Enhance Your Brainpower

Modern-day neuroscience has established that our brain is a far more plastic organ than was previously thought. In the past, it was believed that an adult brain could only lose nerve cells (neurons) and could not acquire new ones. Today we know that new neurons—and new connections between neurons—continue to develop throughout our lives, even well into advanced age. This process is called *neuroplasticity*. Thanks to recent scientific discoveries, we also know that we can harness the powers of neuroplasticity in protecting and even enhancing our minds at every stage of life—including our advanced years.

How can we harness neuroplasticity to help protect and enhance our mental powers? Recent scientific research demonstrates that the brain responds to mental stimulation much like muscles respond to physical exercise. In other words, you have to give your brain a workout. The more vigorous and diverse your mental life—and the more you welcome mental challenges—the more you will stimulate the growth of new neurons and new connections between them. Furthermore, the *nature* of your mental activities influences *where* in the brain this growth takes place. The brain is a very complex organ with different parts in charge of different mental functions. Thus, different cognitive challenges exercise different components of the brain.

How do we know this? We've learned this by combining experiments created from real-life circumstances with *neuroimaging*, the high-resolution technologies that allow scientists to study brain structure and function with amazing precision. Some say that these technologies have done for our understanding of the brain what the invention of the telescope has done for our understanding of the planetary systems. Thanks to these technologies, particularly magnetic resonance imaging (MRI), we know that certain parts of the brain exhibit an increased size in individuals who use these parts of the brain more than most people. For example, researchers found that the hippocampus, a part of the brain critical for spatial memory, was larger than usual in London cab drivers, who have to navigate and remember complex routes in a huge city. Studies revealed that the so-called Heschl's gyrus, a part of the temporal lobe of the brain involved in processing music, is larger in professional musicians than in musically untrained people. And the angular gyrus, the part of the brain involved in language, proved to be larger in bilingual individuals than in those who speak only one language.

What is particularly important is that the size of the effect—the extent to which a specific brain area was enlarged—was directly related to the *amount of time* each person spent in the activities that rely on that brain area.

For instance, the hippocampal size was directly related to the number of years the cab driver spent on the job, and the size of Heschl's gyrus was associated with the amount of time a musician devoted to practicing a musical instrument. This shows that cognitive activity directly influences the structures of the brain by stimulating the effects of neuroplasticity in these structures, since the enlargement of brain regions implies a greater-than-usual number of cells or connections between them. The impact of cognitive activity on the brain can be great enough to result in an actual increase in its size! Indeed, different parts of the brain benefit from certain activities, and the effect can be quite specific.

Diversify Your Mental Workout

It is also true that any more or less complex cognitive function—be it memory, attention, perception, decision making, or problem solving—relies on a whole network of brain regions rather than on a single region. Therefore, any relatively complex mental challenge will engage more than one part of the brain. Yet no single mental activity will engage the whole brain.

This is why the diversity of your mental life is key to your overall brain health. The more vigorous and varied your cognitive challenges, the more efficiently and effectively they'll protect your mind from decline. To return to the workout analogy: Imagine a physical gym. No single exercise machine will make you physically fit. Instead, you need a balanced and diverse workout regime.

You have probably always assumed that crossword puzzles and sudoku are good for you, and they are. But your cognitive workout will benefit more from a greater variety of exercises, particularly if these exercises have been selected with some knowledge of how the brain works.

The puzzle selection for *Brain Games*® has been guided by these considerations—with knowledge of the brain and the roles played by its different parts in the overall orchestra of your mental life. We aimed to assemble as wide a range of puzzles as possible, in order to offer the brain a full workout.

There is no single magic pill to protect or enhance your mind, but vigorous, regular, and diverse mental activity is the closest thing to it. Research indicates that people engaged in mental activities as a result of their education and vocation are less likely to develop dementia as they age. In fact, many of these people demonstrate impressive mental alertness well into their eighties and nineties.

What's more, the "magic pill" need not be bitter. You can engage in activities that are both good for your brain *and* fun. Different kinds of puzzles engage different aspects of your mind, and you can assemble them all into a cognitive workout regime. Variety is the name of the game—that's the whole idea! In each cognitive workout session, have fun by mixing puzzles of different kinds. This book offers you enough puzzle variety to make this possible.

When it comes to difficulty level, welcome challenging puzzles. Don't assume they're beyond your ability without giving them your best shot first. To be effective as a mental workout, the puzzles you choose should not be too easy or too difficult. An overly easy puzzle will not stimulate your brain, just as a leisurely walk in the park is not an efficient way to condition your heart. You need mental exertion. On the other hand, an overly difficult puzzle will just frustrate and discourage you from moving forward. So it is important to find the "challenge zone" that is appropriate for you. This may vary from person to person and from puzzle to puzzle. Here, too, the gym analogy applies. Different people will benefit most from different exercise machines and weight levels.

So we have tried to offer a range of difficulty for the various puzzle types. Try different puzzles to find the starting level appropriate for you. Soon, your puzzle-cracking ability will improve, and you may find that puzzles you once found too hard are now within your grasp.

Have Fun While Stretching Your Mind

The important thing is to have fun while doing something good for you. Puzzles can be engaging, absorbing, and even addictive. An increasing number of people make regular physical exercise part of their daily routines and miss it when circumstances prevent them from exercising. These habitual gym-goers know that strenuous effort is something to look forward to, not to avoid. Similarly, you will strengthen your mental muscle by actively challenging it. Don't put the puzzle book down when the solution is not immediately apparent. By testing your mind, you will discover the joy of a particular kind of accomplishment: watching your mental powers grow. You must have the feeling of mental effort and exertion in order to exercise your brain.

This brings us to the next issue. While all puzzles are good for you, the degree of their effectiveness as brain conditioners is not the same. Some puzzles only test your knowledge of facts. Such puzzles may be enjoyable and useful to a degree, but they're not as effective in conditioning your brain as the puzzles that require you to transform and manipulate information or do something with it by logic, multistep inference, mental rotation, planning, and so on. These latter puzzles are more likely to give you the feeling of mental exertion, of "stretching your mind," and they are also better for your brain health. You can use this feeling as a useful, if inexact, assessment of a puzzle's effectiveness as a brain conditioner.

Try to select puzzles in a way that complements, rather than duplicates, your job-related activities. If your profession involves dealing with words (e.g., an English teacher), try to emphasize spatial puzzles. If you are an engineer dealing with diagrams, focus on verbal puzzles. If your job is relatively devoid of mental challenges of any kind, mix several types of puzzles in equal proportions.

Cognitive decline frequently sets in with aging. It often affects certain kinds of memory and certain aspects of attention and decision making. So as you age, it is particularly important to introduce cognitive exercise into your lifestyle to counteract any possible cognitive decline. But cognitive exercise is also important for the young and the middle-aged. We live in a world that depends increasingly on the brain more than on brawn. It is important to be sharp in order to get ahead in your career and to remain at the top of your game.

How frequently should you exercise your mind and for how long? Think in terms of an ongoing lifestyle change and not just a short-term commitment. Regularity is key, perhaps a few times a week for 30 to 45 minutes at a time. We've tried to make this easier by offering a whole series of *Brain Games*® books. You can carry one of these puzzle books—your "cognitive workout gym"—in your briefcase, backpack, or shopping bag. Our puzzles are intended to be fun, so feel free to fit them into your lifestyle in a way that enhances rather than disrupts it. Research shows that even a relatively brief regimen of vigorous cognitive activity often produces perceptible and lasting effects. But as with physical exercise, the results are best when cognitive exercise becomes a lifelong habit.

To help you gauge your progress, we have included two self-assessment questionnaires: one near the beginning of the book and one near the end. The questionnaires will guide you in rating your various cognitive abilities and any change that you may experience as a result of doing puzzles. Try to be as objective as possible when you fill out the questionnaires. Improving your cognitive skills in real-life situations is the most important practical outcome of exercising your mind, and you are in the best position to note whether and to what extent any improvement has taken place.

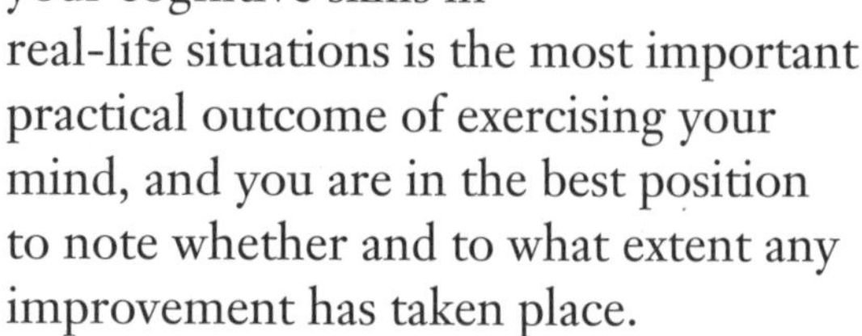

Now that you're aware of the great mental workout that awaits you in this book, we hope that you'll approach these puzzles with a sense of fun. If you have always been a puzzle fan, we offer a great rationale for indulging your passion! You have not been wasting your time by cracking challenging puzzles. Far from it! You have been training and improving your mind.

So, whether you are a new or seasoned puzzle-solver, enjoy your brain workout and get smarter as you go!

ASSESS YOUR BRAIN

You are about to do something very smart: Embark on a set of exercises to improve your mind. But before you begin, take a moment to fill out this self-assessment questionnaire. It is for your own benefit, so you know how well your brain works before you challenge it with *Brain Games*® puzzles. Then you will be able to track any changes in your mental performance and discover the ways in which you have improved.

The questions below are designed to test your skills in the areas of memory, problem solving, creative thinking, attention, language, and more. Please reflect on each question, and rate your abilities on a 5-point scale, where 5 equals "excellent" and 1 equals "very poor." Then tally up your scores, and check out the categories at the bottom of the next page to learn how to sharpen your brain.

1. When you leave your car in a large parking lot for a few hours, how good are you at remembering where you parked? Deduct points if you have to press the remote panic button and listen for the alarm to find your car.

1 2 3 4 5

2. You have to run ten errands at different stores in the same shopping mall. How good are you at planning your trip so that you don't end up criss-crossing the mall several times before you get everything you need?

1 2 3 4 5

3. You've got a busy day at work scheduled, but at the last minute your cat gets sick and you have to take it to the vet. How good are you at juggling your work to accommodate this unanticipated change?

1 2 3 4 5

4. You see an ad in the morning for a new television show that's on the next evening. How likely are you to remember to watch the show?

1 2 3 4 5

5. You're trying to work on an important project, and your coworkers are having a loud meeting next door. How well are you able to block out the distraction to concentrate on the task at hand?

1 2 3 4 5

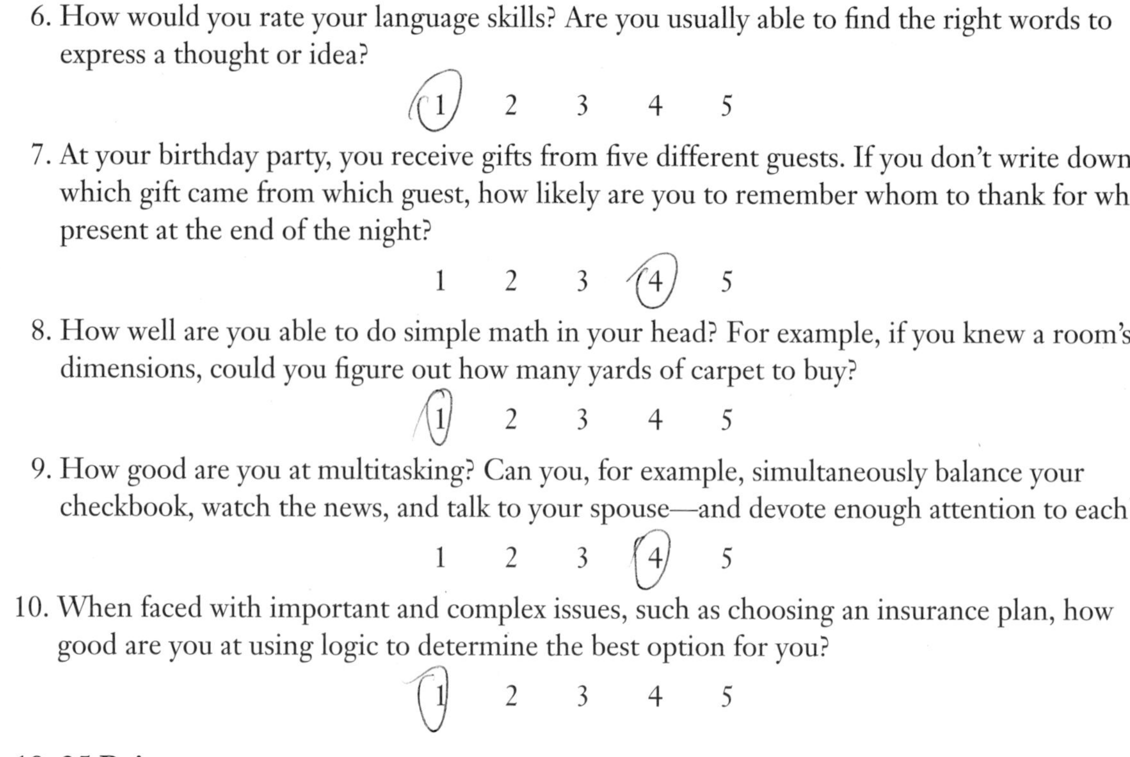

6. How would you rate your language skills? Are you usually able to find the right words to express a thought or idea?

   1 2 3 4 5

7. At your birthday party, you receive gifts from five different guests. If you don't write down which gift came from which guest, how likely are you to remember whom to thank for what present at the end of the night?

   1 2 3 4 5

8. How well are you able to do simple math in your head? For example, if you knew a room's dimensions, could you figure out how many yards of carpet to buy?

   1 2 3 4 5

9. How good are you at multitasking? Can you, for example, simultaneously balance your checkbook, watch the news, and talk to your spouse—and devote enough attention to each?

   1 2 3 4 5

10. When faced with important and complex issues, such as choosing an insurance plan, how good are you at using logic to determine the best option for you?

   1 2 3 4 5

10–25 Points:
Are You Ready to Make a Change?

Remember, it's never too late to improve your brain health! A great way to start is to work puzzles on a regular basis, and you've taken the first step by picking up this book. Choose a different type of puzzle each day, or do a variety of them daily to help strengthen memory, focus attention, and improve logic and problem solving.

26–40 Points:
Building Your Mental Muscle

You're no mental slouch, but there's always room to sharpen your mind! Choose puzzles that will challenge you, especially the types of puzzles you might not like as much or would normally avoid. Remember, doing a puzzle can be the mental equivalent of doing lunges or squats: While they might not be your first choice of activity, you'll definitely like the results!

41–50 Points:
View from the Top

Congratulations! You're keeping your brain in tip-top shape. To maintain this level of mental fitness, keep challenging yourself by working puzzles every day. Like the rest of the body's muscles, your mental strength can decline if you don't use it. So choose to keep your brain strong and active. You're at the summit—now you just have to stay to enjoy the view!

GET FIRED UP!

LEVEL 1

Max and Mitch

LANGUAGE

Oops, we meant *Mix and Match*. But that's what happens when those anagram imps stir up the letters in a word. Can you unscramble the phrases listed below and match the results to their musical pictures?

1. CIRCULATE TIGER
2. HOAX OPENS
3. MOM UTTERED "JAR"
4. IOTA NUMBER
5. A CHARM ION
6. RANCID COO

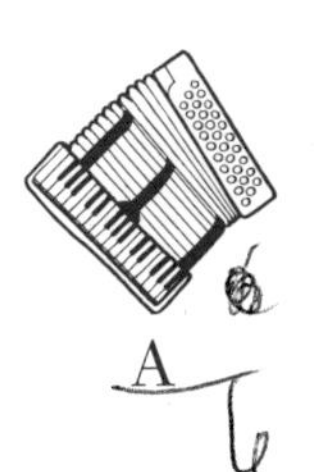
A

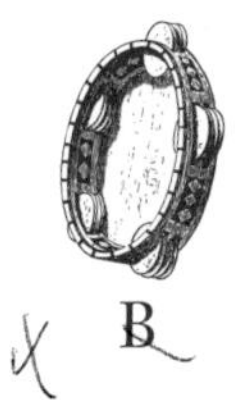
B

C

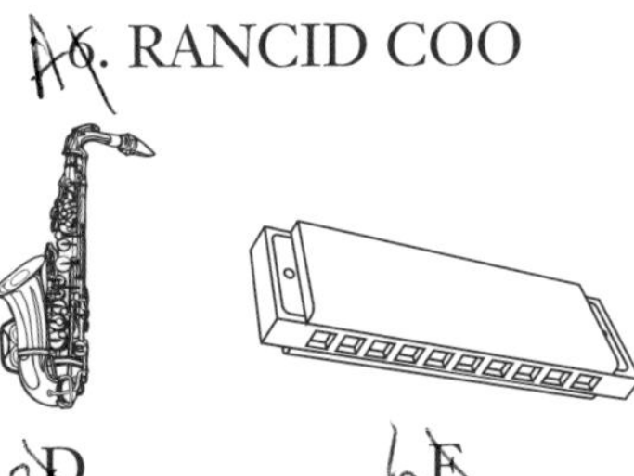
D E

F

Aptagrams

LANGUAGE

What's an aptagram? That's our word for an anagram that is especially apt because the rearranged phrase relates closely to the original word. For example, the letters in ASTRONOMER can be rearranged to create a relevant new phrase: MOON STARER. Get it? Try your hand at these:

1. DIRTY ROOM ________________
2. SO LET'S PINCH ________________
3. HINT: HOTEL ________________
4. LIBERAL BOD ________________

Answers on page 171.

How Long Does It Take?

LANGUAGE LOGIC

Cryptograms are messages in substitution code. Break the code to read the message. For example, THE SMART CAT might become FVO QWGDF JGF if F is substituted for T, V for H, O for E, and so on. The code is the same for each cryptogram in this group.

Hint: Look for repeated letters. E, T, A, O, N, R, and I are the most often used letters. A single letter is usually A or I; OF, IS, and IT are common 2-letter words; THE and AND are common 3-letter words.

1. FH DYY J FPOYY-OQIX LQOLCD: FZH FH FPOYY PHCOD.

2. J TJNNHHI FH SHS: FZH-FPHCDJIKFPD HR J DYLHIK.

3. J TNCY DPJOU FH DZQA J AQNY: HIY AQICFY JIK RHOFB-FPOYY DYLHIKD.

4. J LNHCK FH OYLPJOXY JRFYO NQXPFIQIX RNJDPYD: FZYIFB DYLHIKD.

5. J KJB FH SJDD HI IYSFCIY LHASJOYK FH JI YJOFP KJB: DQWFYYI PHCOD.

Answers on page 171.

Look Before You . . .

LANGUAGE **PLANNING**

Change just one letter on each line to go from the top word to the bottom word. Do not change the order of the letters. You must have a word at each step.

LEAP

HEAP a big pile

HEMP

Hump a camel has one

JUMP

Layer by Layer

LOGIC **SPATIAL VISUALIZATION**

Twelve sheets of paper—all of them equal in size and shape—were piled on a table. Number the sheets from top to bottom, with numbers 1 through 12.

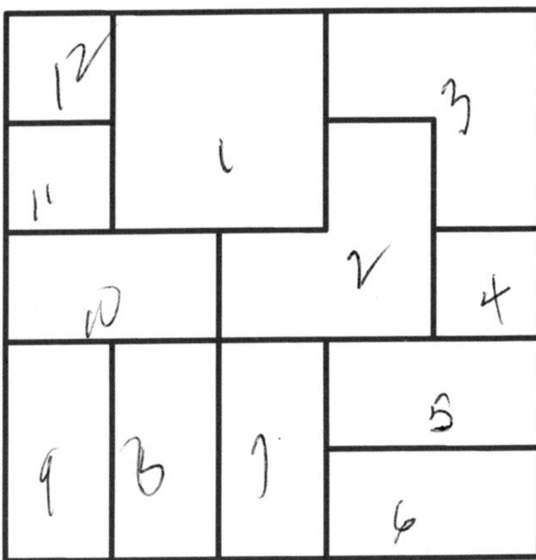

Answers on page 171.

Profit in Baskets

GENERAL KNOWLEDGE | LANGUAGE

Across

1. Carpenter's holder
5. Satellite receiver
9. Chew the fat
12. Publisher Adolph
13. Black and white sandwich
14. A, in Arles
15. Unconscious state
17. Neither Rep. nor Dem.
18. Abduct
19. More nasty
21. T or F, on exams: Abbr.
22. Playground cry
24. ___ noir
25. "The Wizard ___"
26. Irish poet and playwright
27. All profit, in the NBA?
31. Words before "a time"
32. Swiss mountains
33. NY Met, for one
34. Get ready
35. No-goodnik
38. Upper house
40. Danny of "Do the Right Thing"
42. Chiang ___-shek
43. Gift from a bunny
45. Direct ending
46. Land measure
47. Sir's counterpart
48. The, in Berlin
49. Tim of "Sister, Sister"
50. It's figured in square feet

Down

1. Screwdriver ingredient
2. Cause winter isolation
3. Takes off
4. Armchair athlete's channel
5. Miami athlete
6. Rage
7. Terse summons
8. Show optimism
9. Certain African
10. Bening of "American Beauty"
11. Treatment for many illnesses
16. Deemed appropriate
20. Helps during the heist
23. Mystery writers' award
25. Mitchell's Scarlett
26. Modern affluent type
27. Like studded tires
28. Enjoying a furlough
29. More minute
30. Sounded off, like a lamb
34. Type of sign or pipe
35. Like crystal
36. Simple plants
37. Accepted doctrine
39. Pull apart
41. Humorist Bombeck
44. Hindu title

1	2	3	4	■	5	6	7	8	■	9	10	11
12				■	13				■	14		
15				16					■	17		
18						■	19		20			
21			■	22		23		■	24			
■	■	■	25				■	26				
27	28	29					30					
31					■	32				■	■	■
33				■	34				■	35	36	37
38				39		■	40		41			
42			■	43		44						
45			■	46				■	47			
48			■	49				■	50			

Trivia on the Brain

Your soft brain is protected by the bones of your skull. It is also swaddled in several layers of membranes called *meninges.* The fluid between these layers produces a water cushion that helps protect your brain if you bump your head.

Answers on page 171.

Retinue of R's

ATTENTION VISUAL SEARCH

We count 13 things in this picture that begin with the letter R. How many can you find?

Playing the Market

LOGIC

Steve the simple stockbroker owned thousands and thousands of premium shares of stock in the Sterling Silver Silverware company. One day, simple Steve was reading the stock listings in the paper and noticed that his thousands of shares of premium stock were worth much less than they had been the day he bought them. In fact, his shares of the Sterling Silver Silverware Company were almost worthless. Steve wasn't worried though. He could sell all of his holdings and still be a millionaire.

How was this possible?

Answers on page 171.

Fitting Words

LANGUAGE PLANNING

In this miniature crossword, the clues are listed randomly and are numbered for convenience only. It is up to you to figure out the placement of the 9 answers. To help you out, we've inserted one letter in the grid, and this is the *only* occurrence of that letter in the completed puzzle.

Clues

1. Capital city of France
2. Member of a cast
3. Learning method
4. _____ and carrots
5. Vassal
6. Ledge
7. Curved part of the foot
8. Wear away
9. False god

			I	

Sudoku

LOGIC

To solve a sudoku puzzle, place the numbers 1 through 9 in some order in each row, column, and 3×3 box. Each puzzle has some numbers filled in—you just need to work out the rest. You'll never have to guess; the puzzle can be solved using the power of deduction.

		8			9	4		7
4		5	1	6				
	1							6
6	9	2	7	8		3		4
	5						7	
3		4		9	5	2	8	1
5							6	
				7	4	8		3
9		7	2			1		

Answers on page 171.

Geometric Shapes

PLANNING | SPATIAL VISUALIZATION

Divide the grid into smaller geometric shapes by drawing straight lines following either the full grid lines or the full diagonals of the square cells. Each formed shape must have exactly one symbol inside, which represents it but might not look identical to it. (In other words, a triangle you draw must have only a triangle symbol within it, although the drawn triangle and the triangle symbol may look slightly different.) When the puzzle is solved, all of the grid will be used. Hint: The trapezoid has two sides parallel, but its other two sides are not parallel.

Rhyme Time

GENERAL KNOWLEDGE | LANGUAGE

Answer each clue below with a pair of rhyming words. The numbers that follow each clue indicate how many letters are in each word. For example, "Cookware taken straight from the oven (3, 3)" would be "hot pot."

1. Assessment on telecopy usage (3, 3): ______________________
2. Make a change at the bakery (3, 3): ______________________
3. Next to fly the plane (3, 4): ______________________
4. Traded in a precious metal (4, 4): ______________________
5. Teak (4, 4): ______________________
6. Stain, sometimes (4, 4): ______________________
7. Use the microwave to warm steak (4, 4): ______________________
8. Ideal spouse (5, 4): ______________________
9. Hurler signing a big contract (6, 7): ______________________
10. Enjoyable game bird (8, 8): ______________________

Answers on page 172.

Soupy Sailfish

PLANNING | SPATIAL REASONING

Answer on page 172.

Cone You Top This?

ATTENTION LANGUAGE VISUAL SEARCH

In the mood for summer weather, picnics, and the ice-cream truck? This word search is just the thing! Every word listed below is contained within the group of letters on the next page. The words can be found horizontally, vertically, or diagonally. They may read either backward or forward.

BARBECUE	HOT DOGS	SIGHTSEEING
BASEBALL	ICE CREAM	SNOW CONE
BOATING	JET SKI	SPRINKLER
BURN	KAYAKING	SUN
CAMPFIRE	LEISURE	SWIMMING
CAMPING	MOTOR HOME	SWING
CANOEING	MOW	TAN
DAYLIGHT	OUTDOORS	TENT
DIVING	PARK	TRAILER
GARDEN	PICNIC	TRIP
GRILL	PLAYGROUND	TUBING
HAMBURGERS	POOL	VACATION
HAMMOCK	POPSICLE	WATERSKIING
HEAT	RAFTING	YARD WORK
HIKING	SAILING	

V T E N T O I G
A K X R Z U W P A D G L
X N A T A E S G L Z A A B T
P G O Y D I R N E A K Y R U S U
U N I A T L I O O Y K L D R Y D
G I T K J E F W B G S I E N O M
P N P A I O R P C B R P G N I V I D
O I M C N E M M O T O R H O M E E T
O B A A G L O A N U U I T Z G R K H
A L U C V Y C T C E B N N Z R U R A T O
T T T L I A W M R D K I S O M P
B B D N S E A O R C L I W M I P
S G G O P H T W P L E D O C G P
W N A O A E I Q L R C N N L
I I P R R N O A K I I B
N M T S K Y B C E T
G M K C J E E U
N X I G E S G C
I K I W T A N E
L L N H S B I B
I S G B K Y K R
A I M J I N I A
S G O D T O H B
G N I T F A R B
J E P N V M R B

Answers on page 172.

Mirror, Mirror

SPATIAL VISUALIZATION

There's no trick here, only a challenge: Draw the mirror image of each of these familiar objects. You may find it harder than you think!

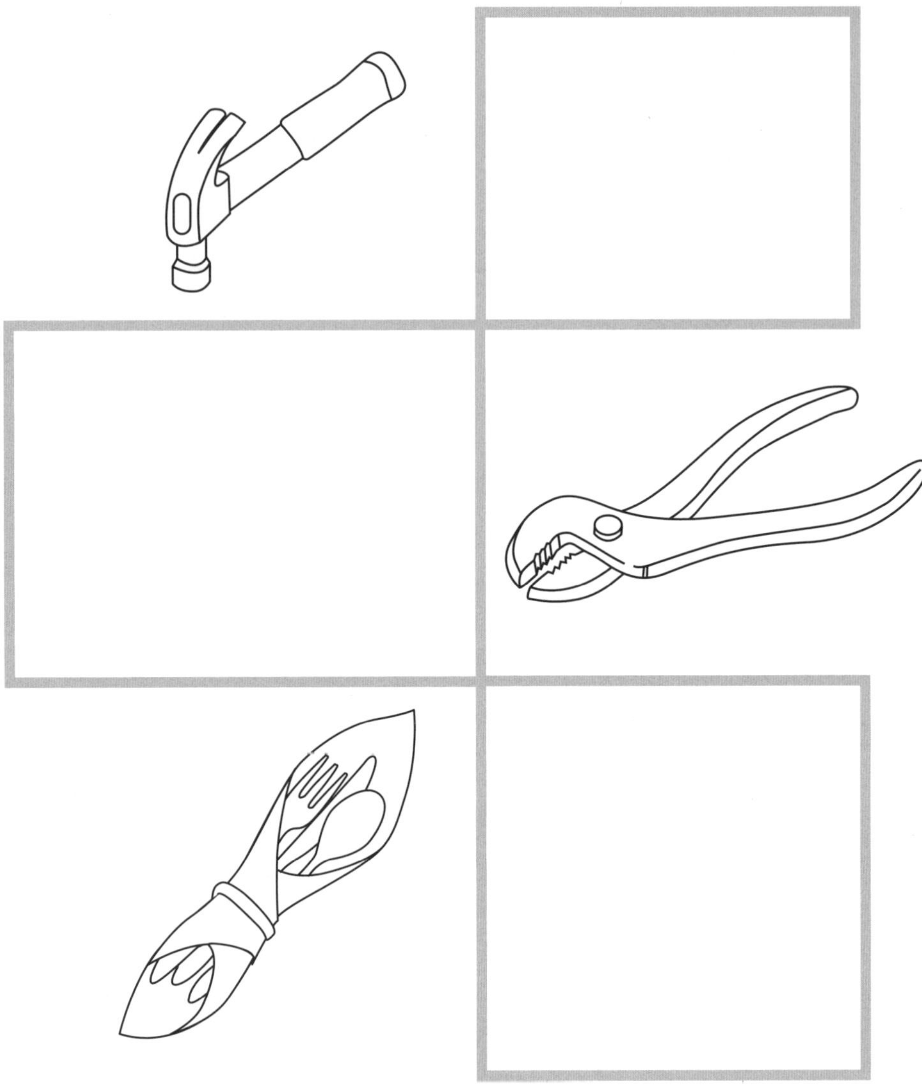

Where Are the Animals?

LANGUAGE

Find the names of 2 animals in each group of letters. The letters in each name are in their proper order. We've done one for you.

1. DOCAGT ____DOG____ ____CAT____
2. SEKLUNKK ________ ________
3. DEOWERL ________ ________
4. FOSNAXKE ________ ________
5. WHOORLSEF ________ ________
6. RELAEBPHABINTT ________ ________
7. TILIGONER ________ ________
8. MEONAGKLEYE ________ ________
9. SWEHAALLE ________ ________
10. PEAREROLT ________ ________

Trivia on the Brain

Your mind is basically a seven-pound ball of malleable flesh. Every bit of it crackles with billions of little switches called *synapses.* These are the points at which your brain's nerve cells exchange ions. We call this "thinking." The more synaptic connections you form in your mind, the more you know. As you age, these connections begin to fray. We call this "forgetting."

Answers on page 172.

The Shading Game

ATTENTION | VISUAL SEARCH

Use a pencil or highlighter to shade all of the squares that contain the numeral **3.** The shaded area will spell out the answer to this riddle: What did the baseball player do when he couldn't hit right?

4	5	1	9	8	2	4	1	0	8	7	6	0	7	4
7	6	3	4	3	8	7	3	1	9	3	3	3	7	8
2	9	3	1	3	5	5	3	6	7	5	3	9	8	1
8	4	3	3	3	7	8	3	4	5	2	3	2	2	9
6	4	3	5	3	4	9	3	6	0	7	3	2	7	8
7	9	3	4	3	7	7	3	2	0	4	3	1	5	6
5	0	9	1	4	2	7	6	8	7	1	9	4	6	4
6	4	5	8	7	1	2	2	9	9	0	7	1	5	7
3	5	6	2	3	3	3	9	3	3	3	7	3	3	3
3	7	6	9	3	5	6	2	3	7	6	9	8	3	4
3	4	1	7	3	3	8	7	3	3	2	1	5	3	4
3	9	8	5	3	2	4	1	3	6	5	7	9	3	0
3	3	3	6	3	3	3	1	3	4	5	9	2	3	7
5	6	5	9	8	1	2	0	4	6	5	8	1	9	7
6	6	9	1	8	2	4	2	2	0	9	8	1	7	5

Answer on page 172.

It's Tricky!, Part I

ATTENTION | VISUAL SEARCH

Jocko the Magnificent is a great magician, but he has a problem: He doesn't always remember which props he uses in his magic act. See if you can help.

First, study this picture for two minutes. Then turn the page for a quiz on what you've seen.

Many Mice

ATTENTION | LANGUAGE | VISUAL SEARCH

Ignoring spaces and punctuation, how many occurrences of the consecutive letters M-I-C-E can you find in the paragraph below?

Tami centered the ceramic egg that Mick eventually gave her so she wouldn't miss him while he worked for the Atomic Energy Commission. Tami smoothed the egg with a pumice stone, the only one in her domicile. Tami enjoyed the egg, but Mick's gift of an imported salami cemented their relationship and helped her to miss him less.

Answer on page 172.

It's Tricky!, Part II

MEMORY

(Do not read this until you have read the previous page!)

Three of the props pictured here belong to another magician and did NOT appear on the preceding page. From memory, can you figure out which ones they are?

Crypto-Wisdom

LANGUAGE LOGIC

Cryptograms are messages in substitution code. Break the code to read the message. For example, THE SMART CAT might become FVO QWGDF JGF if F is substituted for T, V for H, O for E, and so on. The code is the same for each cryptogram in this group.

Hint: Look for repeated letters. E, T, A, O, N, R, and I are the most often used letters. A single letter is usually A or I; OF, IS, IT, THE, and AND are common letter groups.

1. I JGHHEKF MNGKC FINLCJM KG OGMM.

2. I BCKKP MISCA EM I BCKKP CIJKCA.

3. DEKA RGJAM HEKFCJ EK NLC LCIJN.

Answers on page 172.

Read Between the Lines

LANGUAGE LOGIC

Solve for the middle (undefined) word in each set. All 3 words in each set can be found on the same page in the dictionary, **in the order they appear here**. By figuring out what the first and third words are, you should be able to identify the middle word. Take the middle words from each group and arrange them to complete the quote below. **Note:** You'll need to add an **S** to 3 different words to complete the quote.

Example: a) p u t t e r : to work at random; tinker

b) p u z z l e

c) p y g m y : one of a race of dwarfs

1. a) _ _ m m _ _ _ : any of numerous extinct Pleistocene elephants

   b) _ _ _

   c) _ _ _ _ _ l _ : a shackle for the hand or wrist

2. a) _ _ m p u _ : a usually noisy commotion

   b) r _ _

   c) _ _ _ a _ _ _ : a fugitive

3. a) _ _ _ _ _ _ _ _ _ p t : a document written by hand or typed, as opposed to printed

   b) _ _ n y

   c) _ _ p : a representation of an area of land or sea

4. a) _ _ s _ _ : the upright member between two stair treads

   b) _ _ s _

   c) _ _ _ q _ _: verging on impropriety or indecency

5. a) _ _ s t _ _ : a female having the same parents as another person

   b) _ i _

   c) _ _ _ a _ : an Indian lute

"A __________ __________ as __________ __________ as he __________."

—Henry David Thoreau

Answers on page 172.

Flying High

LANGUAGE

Unscramble the names of these common birds, then use the numbered squares to solve the second puzzle, a related idiom.

Scrambled	Boxes	Numbered squares
COANFL	6 boxes	1 (box 1)
RIOBN	5 boxes	8 (box 3)
CAALINRD	8 boxes	7 (box 2), 11 (box 4)
NAARYC	6 boxes	10 (box 5)
BIRDULEB	8 boxes	4 (box 4)
WOCR	4 boxes	2 (box 2)
EGLAE	5 boxes	3 (box 5)
WSROPRA	7 boxes	5 (box 3)
GASLIRNT	8 boxes	6 (box 1), 9 (box 6)

1 2 3 4   5 6   7   8 9 10 11

Answers on page 173.

Assemblage of A's

ATTENTION | VISUAL SEARCH

Within this picture is an assemblage of things beginning with the letter **A.** We count 15. How many can you find?

Rectangle Census

PERCEPTION | SPATIAL REASONING

How many rectangles are formed by the lines in this diagram? Although there are fewer than 15 rectangles, many people count incorrectly when they try this puzzle. How will you do?

Hint: Label each separate region of the diagram with a letter and make a list of letter combinations that form rectangles.

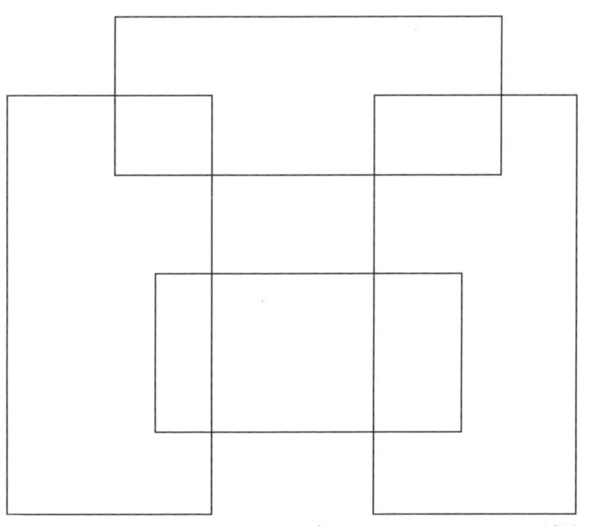

Answers on page 173.

You Auto Like This

ATTENTION LANGUAGE VISUAL SEARCH

Every word listed below is contained within the box of letters on the next page. The words can be found in a straight line horizontally, vertically, or diagonally. They may read either backward or forward.

AIR BAGS
ALARM
ANTENNA
AXLE
BODY
BRAKES
BULB
CARBURETOR
CLUTCH
DASHBOARD
DOORS
ENGINE
FENDER
FILTER
FRAME
GASKET
GAUGE
GEARS
GRILLE
HEADLIGHT
HOOD
HORN
HOSE
LAMP
LOCKS
MATS
MIRROR
MUFFLER
PANELS
PEDALS
PUMP
RADIO
RODS
SEAT BELTS
SPEEDOMETER
SUNROOF
TACHOMETER
TIRES
WHEEL
WIPERS

T	Z	A	B	O	D	Y	M	A	N	N	E	T	N	A
A	E	L	L	I	R	G	E	S	O	H	D	R	S	I
C	Y	A	U	D	A	S	H	B	O	A	R	D	F	R
H	E	R	B	A	S	K	K	O	V	J	O	O	O	B
O	G	M	L	R	R	L	D	C	R	R	Q	O	O	A
M	U	F	F	L	E	R	M	X	O	N	V	R	R	G
E	A	P	M	U	P	T	J	T	W	L	H	S	N	S
T	G	Z	C	Z	I	R	E	D	N	E	F	H	U	T
E	A	Q	E	L	W	R	R	M	A	M	I	B	S	L
R	S	P	M	E	U	T	A	D	O	J	L	C	L	E
O	K	E	A	B	N	T	L	Z	G	D	T	G	E	B
R	E	D	R	Y	S	I	C	A	X	L	E	P	N	T
R	T	A	F	Z	G	G	G	H	M	A	R	E	A	A
I	C	L	W	H	E	E	L	N	R	P	L	Y	P	E
M	R	S	T	I	R	E	S	S	E	K	A	R	B	S

Trivia on the Brain

The brain contains as many neurons as there are stars in the Milky Way.

Answers on page 173.

Cheer Up!

LANGUAGE PLANNING

Change just one letter on each line to go from the top word to the bottom word. Do not change the order of the letters. You must put a common English word at each step.

SAD

______

______

JOY

Word Jigsaw

SPATIAL PLANNING

Fit the pieces into the frame to form common, uncapitalized words reading across and down crossword-style. There's no need to rotate the pieces; they'll fit as shown, with each piece used exactly once.

N E

R E

N D

T I

I / E

I / P

A / B

A / T

Answers on page 173.

Fish Fantasy

ATTENTION VISUAL SEARCH

This tank is just swimming with fish. Can you find the 2 that match?

Answer on page 173.

Max and Mitch Strike Again

LANGUAGE

Those anagram imps like nothing better than stirring up letters in a word—just to drive you crazy. Unscramble the phrases, then match them to the correct pictures.

1. ICY FEMALES
2. DO ALONG
3. CLEAN HOME
4. GOLD LORY

A

B

C

D

Geometric Shapes

PLANNING

SPATIAL VISUALIZATION

Divide the grid into smaller geometric shapes by drawing straight lines that follow either the full grid lines or the full diagonals of the square cells. Each formed shape must have exactly one symbol inside, which represents it but might not look identical to it. (In other words, a triangle you draw must have only a triangle symbol in it, although the drawn triangle and the triangle symbol may look slightly different.) Hints: The rectangle symbol cannot be contained in a square. The parallelogram is not inside a rectangle or a square. The trapezoid has two sides parallel, but its other two sides are not parallel.

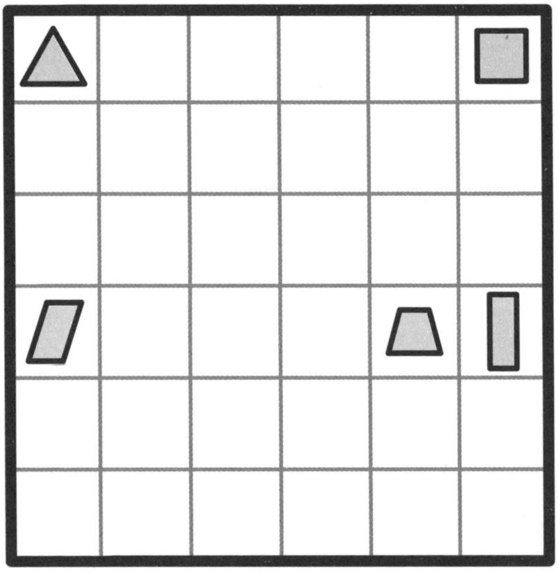

Answers on page 173.

Continuous Line Bet

PLANNING

Draw 4 straight lines to bisect each of these circles. Do not lift your pencil from the page. Do not double back.

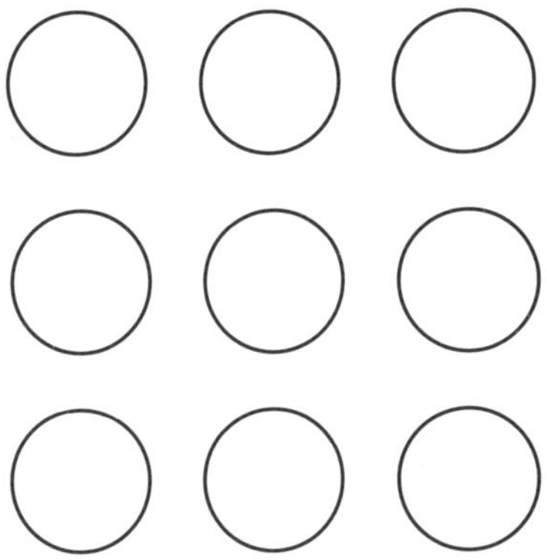

Honeycomb

ATTENTION VISUAL SEARCH

There are 16 letters in the honeycomb below that are surrounded by 6 different letters (no letters are repeated). Can you find them all?

Answers on page 174.

Mirror, Mirror

SPATIAL VISUALIZATION

There's no trick here, only a challenge: Draw the mirror image of each of these familiar objects. You may find it harder than you think!

Fitting Words

LANGUAGE PLANNING

In this miniature crossword, the clues are listed randomly and are numbered for convenience only. It is up to you to figure out the placement of the 9 answers. To help you out, we've inserted one letter in the grid, and this is the *only* occurrence of that letter in the completed puzzle.

Clues

1. Tale
2. Make carpets
3. Always
4. Classroom book
5. Outdo
6. Bank (on)
7. Is in debt
8. Mexican snack
9. Playful river critter

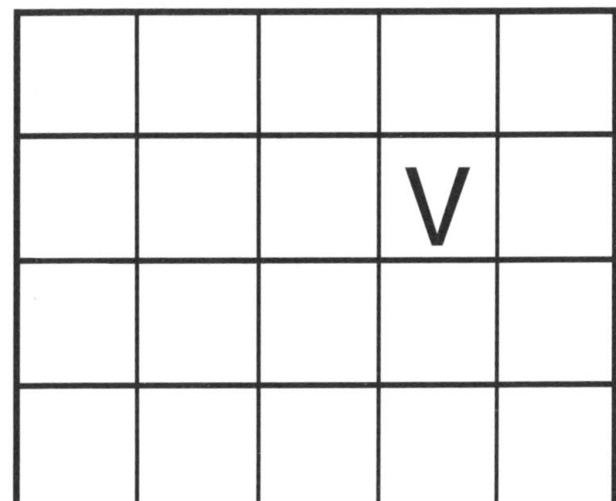

Word Jigsaw

SPATIAL PLANNING

Fit the pieces into the frame to form common, uncapitalized words reading across and down crossword-style. There's no need to rotate the pieces; they'll fit as shown, with each piece used exactly once.

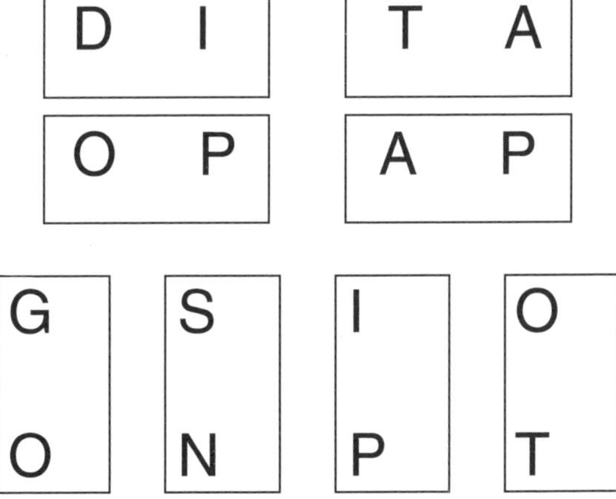

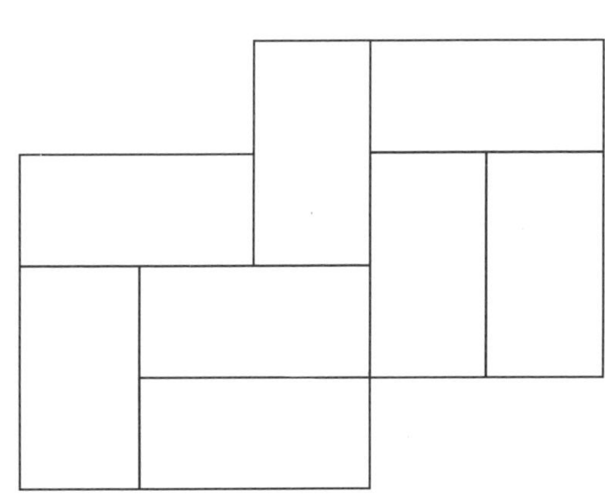

Answers on page 174.

Let's Get Away from It All

GENERAL KNOWLEDGE LANGUAGE

Across

1. Bio and chem, e.g.
5. British nobleman
9. Man of morals?
14. Sighed words
15. Medical picture
16. Courageous
17. Early television situation comedy: 4 wds.
20. Other than
21. Jealousy
22. Before, poetically
23. Infamous Roman emperor
25. Mt. Rushmore's state: abbr.
27. Sleep state, for short
30. Merit
32. Busybodies
36. Medical school subj.: abbr.
38. New corp. hires
40. Editor's mark
41. "Get lost!"
44. Dangerous bacteria
45. Scarlett's plantation
46. Skin cream additive
47. Like a high-pitched scream
49. Spinnaker, for one
51. Sunday talk: abbr.
52. Commoner
54. Shawl or stole
56. Salty expanse
59. "_____ to please!": 2 wds.
61. Enchants
65. "Come in, stay a while!"
68. Japanese, perhaps
69. Campus club, commonly
70. Simple melody
71. Leases
72. _____ Fifth Avenue
73. Observes

Down

1. Mall attraction
2. General Mills cereal
3. Apple computer product
4. Lucky number, for some
5. Highway egress: 2 wds.
6. Sculpture or dance
7. $10/hour, say
8. French silk center
9. Temporary suspension
10. Important time period
11. Use a piggy bank
12. Above
13. Pierre's pop
18. Blunted sword
19. Some briefs, briefly
24. Planet's path
26. Australian eucalyptus eater
27. Rants and raves
28. Methuselah's father
29. Of prime importance
31. Grannies

33. Tough exams
34. Tea type
35. Beef source
37. Bloom associated with Holland
39. Barn floor covering
42. A great deal
43. Salon offerings
48. Bit of foliage
50. Cowardly Lion portrayer
53. Punches
55. Formal agreements
56. Play the lead
57. Abate
58. Similar (to)
60. Pianist Hess
62. Lecher
63. Lion's locks
64. French holy women: abbr.
66. Chow down
67. Acorn's future identity

Answers on page 174.

Rhyme Time

GENERAL KNOWLEDGE | LANGUAGE

Answer each clue below with a pair of rhyming words. The numbers that follow each clue indicate how many letters are in each word. For example, "Cookware taken straight from the oven (3, 3)" would be "hot pot."

1. Smoked salmon purchase (3, 3): ______________________
2. Take care of the parrot (4, 4): ______________________
3. Mild expletive about a farm building (4, 4): ______________________
4. It hurts most of all (4, 4): ______________________
5. Ingot shaper (4, 4): ______________________
6. Offer at a seafood auction (5, 3): ______________________
7. Bakery emanation (5, 5): ______________________
8. It caused the gymnast to get a 7 (5, 5): ______________________
9. Young girl's outer garment (5, 5): ______________________
10. Prepare for the poetry recital (8, 5): ______________________

No Buts About It!

ATTENTION | LANGUAGE | VISUAL SEARCH

Ignoring spaces and punctuation, how many occurrences of the consecutive letters B-U-T can you find in the paragraph below?

Bob, a bubba from Old Knob, Utah, stole butter from a butcher and was sentenced to jail. "I made a booboo," Bob uttered to the judge, but the judge said, "Bob, Utica is the prison for thieves like you." "But, but!" stammered Tab, underpaid attorney for Bob. "Utica is bad for butter thieves." "No ifs, ands, or buts," rebutted the judge. "Bob, Utica awaits your debut as a prisoner tomorrow." Bob, turning to his beautiful gal Bab, uttered, "Buh-bye."

Answers on page 174.

It's a Jungle (of Numbers!) Out There

ATTENTION | VISUAL SEARCH

This cityscape is loaded with hidden numbers. How many can you find?

Answer on page 174.

Rhyme Time

GENERAL KNOWLEDGE LANGUAGE

Answer each clue below with a pair of rhyming words. The numbers that follow each clue indicate how many letters are in each word. For example, "Cookware taken straight from the oven (3, 3)" would be "hot pot."

1. Easy one-mile jog along the beach (3, 3): ____________________
2. Not enough (3, 3): ____________________
3. Legal loophole (3, 4): ____________________
4. Elvis's was suede (4, 4): ____________________
5. Entertaining stunt (4, 4): ____________________
6. Barbecue meat (4, 5): ____________________
7. Licorice (5, 5): ____________________
8. Robin Hood, for one (5, 5): ____________________
9. Where to buy a surfboard (5, 5): ____________________
10. Waves (5, 6): ____________________

The Great Escape

LOGIC

Ivan was an extremely dangerous bank robber imprisoned at a maximum security prison. Ivan spent 24 hours a day 20 feet from the prison wall attached to one end of a 15-foot chain made from industrial-strength steel. In spite of this, Ivan still managed to climb the wall and go back to robbing banks. How did he escape?

Answers on page 174.

Make a Match

LANGUAGE

Decipher the anagrams below, then match them to the pictures.

1. HISSED A LITTLE
2. DEBITS HURT
3. FINISHED
4. CHAD FISHING

A

B

C

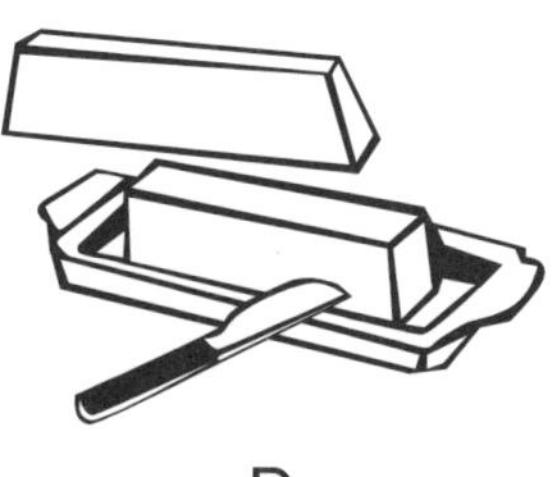

D

Trivia on the Brain

Amino acids from proteins are used to make the neurotransmitters that enable your brain cells to network and communicate.

Essentially, fats build your brain, and proteins unite the cells. Carbohydrates fuel your brain, and micronutrients defend it.

Answers on page 174.

XOXO

ATTENTION LOGIC PLANNING

Write either an X or an O inside each empty cell of the grid so the same letter does not appear in 4 consecutive cells horizontally, vertically, or diagonally.

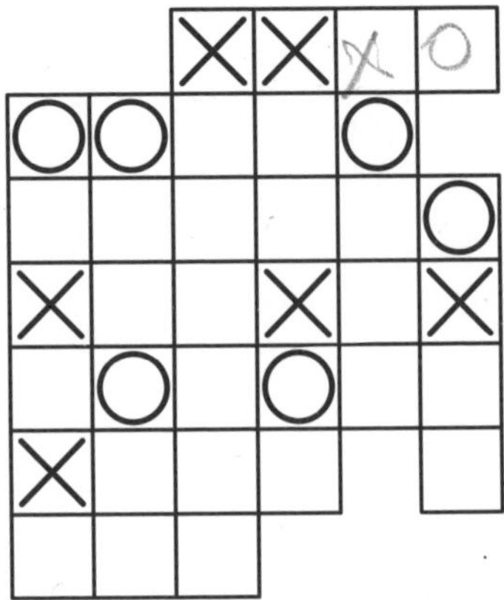

We Shall Over...Come

LANGUAGE PLANNING

How many steps does it take to get from OVER to COME? We needed 8, as shown below. Can you use the clues we've provided to retrace the steps we took? Remember: You must have a common English word at each step.

OVER

_______ At all

_______ Dec. 24 and Dec. 31

_______ Sees things?

_______ Easter egg colors, for example

_______ Acts

_______ Morse units

_______ Mollycoddle, with "on"

_______ Capitol topper

COME

Answers on page 175.

Let's Make Some Music

LANGUAGE LOGIC PLANNING

The letters in the word UKULELE can be found in boxes 12, 16, 19, and 22, but not necessarily in that order. Similarly, the letters in all the other listed musical instruments can be found in the boxes indicated. Your task is to insert all the letters into the grid. If you do this correctly, the names of 2 more instruments will be revealed in the shaded squares.

Hint: Compare BANJO and BASSOON to get the values of J and S. Then compare BASSOON and DOUBLE BASS to get the value of N.

BANJO: 5, 6, 7, 8, 21

BASSOON: 5, 6, 7, 20, 21

DOUBLE BASS: 5, 7, 14, 16, 19, 20, 21, 22

FLUTE: 10, 13, 16, 19, 22

OCARINA: 4, 5, 6, 7, 15, 23

ORGAN: 1, 5, 6, 7, 15

PICCOLO: 3, 4, 7, 19, 23

SAXOPHONE: 2, 3, 5, 6, 7, 11, 20, 22

TIN WHISTLE: 2, 4, 6, 9, 10, 19, 20, 22

TRUMPET: 3, 10, 15, 16, 17, 22

UKULELE: 12, 16, 19, 22

VIOLA: 4, 5, 7, 19, 24

XYLOPHONE: 2, 3, 6, 7, 11, 19, 22, 25

ZITHER: 2, 4, 10, 15, 18, 22

1	2	3	4	5	6	7	8	9	10	11	12	13
14	15	16	17	18	19	20	21	22	23	24	25	26
												Q

Answers on page 175.

Number Crossword

COMPUTATION LOGIC

Use the clues to determine which of the digits 1 through 9 belongs in each square in the diagram. Digits may be repeated within a number, and no zeros are used.

Across

1. A multiple of 3
3. Four identical odd digits
5. Consecutive digits, ascending
6. An even number

Down

1. A palindrome
2. A perfect square
3. A prime number
4. Nine more than 3-Down

Fitting Words

LANGUAGE LOGIC PLANNING

In this miniature crossword, the clues are listed randomly and are numbered for convenience only. It is up to you to figure out the placement of the 9 answers. To help you out, we've inserted one letter in the grid, and this is the *only* occurrence of that letter in the completed puzzle.

Clues

1. Magazine-stand choice
2. Screen dot
3. Past, for example
4. Otherwise
5. Yoked team
6. Signs
7. Friendly dog
8. Contact
9. Took

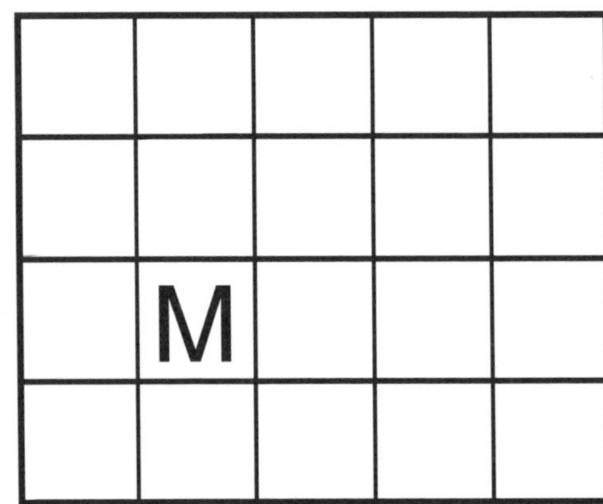

Answers on page 175.

Zone of Z's

ATTENTION VISUAL SEARCH

Inside this picture is a zone of things beginning with the letter **Z.** We count 8 things. How many can you find?

Answers on page 175.

Spark Your Mind

Hurry!

GENERAL KNOWLEDGE | LANGUAGE

Across

1. Wild guess
5. Mont Blanc, for example
8. Did in
12. Columbus's home
13. Civil War general
14. Scruff
15. "Hurry!"
17. Like
18. One for the books?
19. Facet
21. Frittata
23. Circumspect
27. Small Pacific salmons
31. Aptly named fruit
32. Slow-witted
34. Presidential caucus state
35. Dark meat choice
37. Bread crumbs, perhaps
39. Like last-minute chores, often
41. Small bar
44. Kind of report
49. First place?
50. "Hurry!"
52. Matador's opponent
53. Sensitive subject, to some
54. Writer Ferber
55. Side order
56. Heir, perhaps
57. 49-across inhabitant

Down

1. Counter order
2. Friends' pronoun
3. Isn't incorrect?
4. Two out of two
5. Worried, and then some
6. Maui memento
7. Corolla part
8. "Hurry!"
9. Superior, for one
10. Like a De Mille production
11. Left
16. Club choice
20. Dry, as champagne
22. Ruler's decree
23. Kind of instinct
24. "That's disgusting"
25. Baba of "Arabian Nights"
26. "Hurry!"
28. ___ polloi
29. Fess (up)
30. Droop
33. Wet a little
36. Part of H.M.S.
38. Book after John
40. Counter orders
41. Wagers
42. Superstar
43. Immunizing stuff
45. Word with code or rug
46. Mary Lincoln, née ___
47. Arm bone
48. Bridge coup
51. Pride

1	2	3	4	■	5	6	7	■	8	9	10	11
12				■	13			■	14			
15				16				■	17			
18						■	19	20				
■	■	■	■	21		22				■	■	■
23	24	25	26				■	27		28	29	30
31				■	32		33	■	34			
35				36	■	37		38				
■	■	■	39		40				■	■	■	■
41	42	43				■	44		45	46	47	48
49				■	50	51						
52				■	53			■	54			
55				■	56			■	57			

Trivia on the Brain

Your brain stem connects your brain to your spinal cord. It is responsible for regulating many life-support mechanisms, such as breathing, blood pressure, and digestion.

Answers on page 175.

Mirror, Mirror

SPATIAL VISUALIZATION

There's no trick here, only a challenge: Draw the mirror image of each of these familiar objects. You may find it harder than you think!

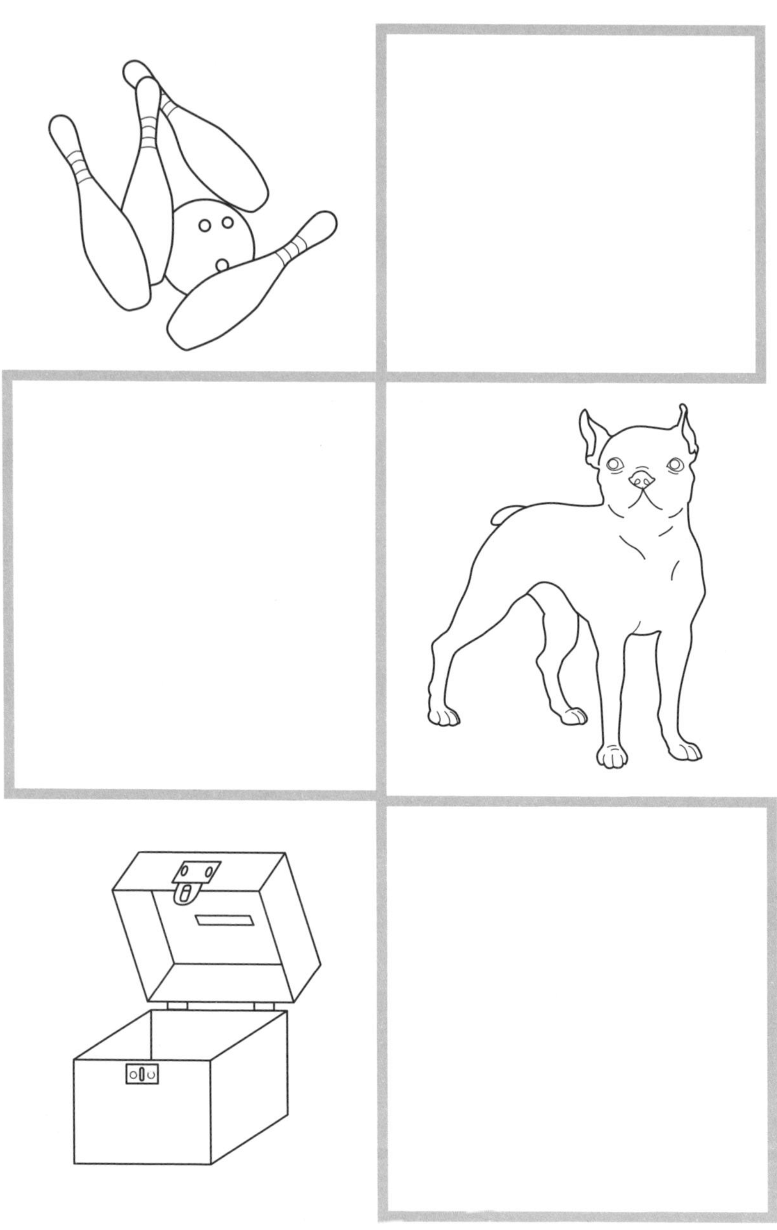

Crazy Mixed-Up Letters

LANGUAGE

Make 3 different 7-letter words by rearranging all of the letters shown here.

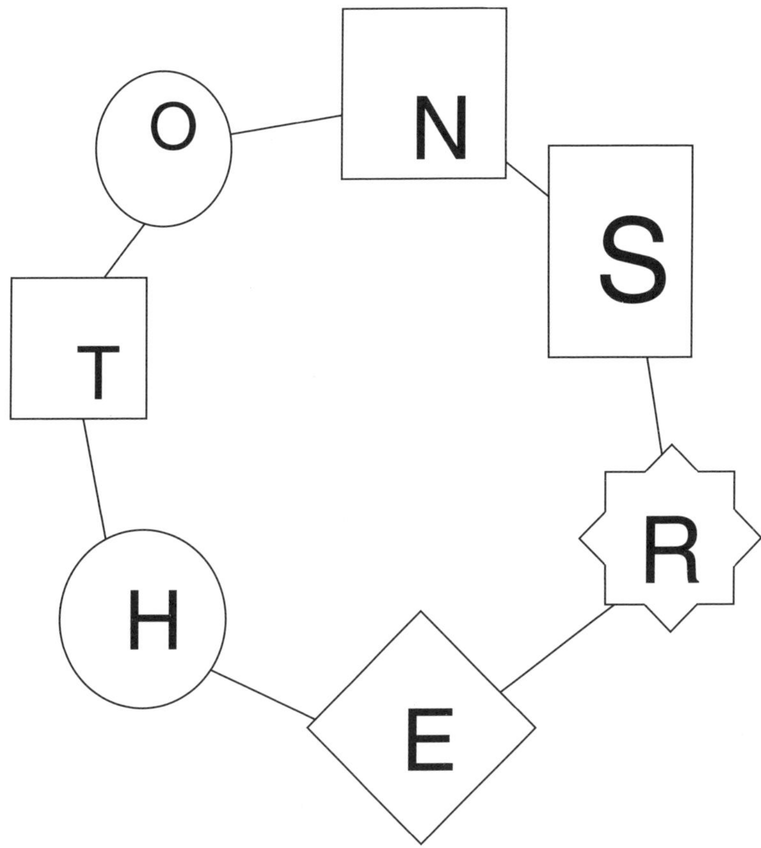

Trivia on the Brain

Your amygdala is your brain's alarm system. Depending on which area is stimulated, your body will experience either a "fight" response or a "flight" response.

Answers on page 175.

Tag! You're It!

ANALYSIS | CREATIVE THINKING

Can you determine the next letter in this progression?

E M M ___

Sudoku

LOGIC

To solve a sudoku puzzle, place the numbers 1 through 9 in some order in each row, column, and 3×3 box. Each puzzle has some numbers filled in—you just need to work out the rest. You'll never have to guess; the puzzle can be solved using only the power of deduction.

		9	7	2				
1	4		6	5				
7		6	8		9			
2	9					7	8	
	6						4	
	1	4					2	9
			3		6	9		8
				8	7		3	6
				9	5	1		

Answers on page 175.

Circus Time

ATTENTION LANGUAGE VISUAL SEARCH

Every word listed is contained within this box of letters. The words can be found horizontally, vertically, or diagonally. They may read either backward or forward.

S	S	T	S	I	L	A	I	R	E	A	R	E	I	R
T	I	G	H	T	R	O	P	E	N	G	Z	S	I	E
N	I	R	E	K	R	A	B	T	L	E	I	N	R	W
A	N	G	N	G	R	B	R	S	P	O	G	W	E	O
H	R	T	E	A	L	B	E	A	R	S	H	O	D	R
P	O	S	D	R	I	I	R	M	F	T	M	L	I	H
E	C	E	I	G	S	T	O	G	E	A	E	C	R	T
L	P	R	T	D	G	S	B	N	G	P	T	S	K	E
E	O	O	M	N	E	A	T	I	T	E	T	M	C	F
R	P	N	I	U	M	S	C	R	A	A	N	D	A	I
B	A	Y	D	L	S	S	H	I	B	N	M	L	B	N
Y	L	T	W	E	L	H	E	O	E	U	G	E	E	K
F	R	E	A	A	T	A	R	B	W	T	E	S	R	T
S	H	L	Y	O	W	C	C	O	U	S	N	E	A	A
R	S	T	Y	D	A	L	D	E	D	R	A	E	B	H

ACROBATS
AERIALISTS
BAREBACK RIDER
BARKER
BEARDED LADY
BEARS
BIG TOP
CALLIOPE
CLOWNS
ELEPHANTS
FAT MAN
FLYING TRAPEZE
KNIFE THROWER
LION TAMER
MAGIC
MIDWAY
PARADE
PEANUTS
POPCORN
RINGMASTER
RINGS
RUBES
SEALS
SIDESHOWS
TENTS
TIGERS
TIGHTROPE

Answers on page 175.

Rhyme Time

GENERAL KNOWLEDGE | LANGUAGE

Answer each clue below with a pair of rhyming words. The numbers that follow each clue indicate how many letters are in each word. For example, "Cookware taken straight from the oven (3, 3)" would be "hot pot."

1. Every fast-food outlet's offering (4, 4): ____________________
2. Landscapers' promo (4, 4): ____________________
3. It started at 11:00 P.M. (4, 4): ____________________
4. Obsessive surfer (4, 5): ____________________
5. It may be set by the college coach (4, 4): ____________________
6. Hometown fans' desire (4, 5): ____________________
7. Evidence of fans' desire fulfilled (4, 5): ____________________
8. Top-ranked quarterback (5, 4): ____________________
9. Sweet-shop attraction (5, 5): ____________________
10. They won in a landslide (5, 5): ____________________
11. He won the title at age 65 (5, 5): ____________________
12. It blocks river traffic (5, 5): ____________________
13. Multipurpose lawn tool (6, 5): ____________________
14. Bad-tempered Bronx pro (6, 6): ____________________
15. Run-of-the-mill prom dress (6, 6): ____________________

Answers on page 176.

See Your Name in Print!

SPATIAL REASONING

This puzzle is so amazing we can hardly catch our breath. Merely put the letter parts together, and they'll spell your name! Sorry, we can't reveal the amazing 23rd-century technology behind this wizardry. Oh, yes, one or more letter parts may have been rotated—a small obstacle to the fun of seeing your name in print!

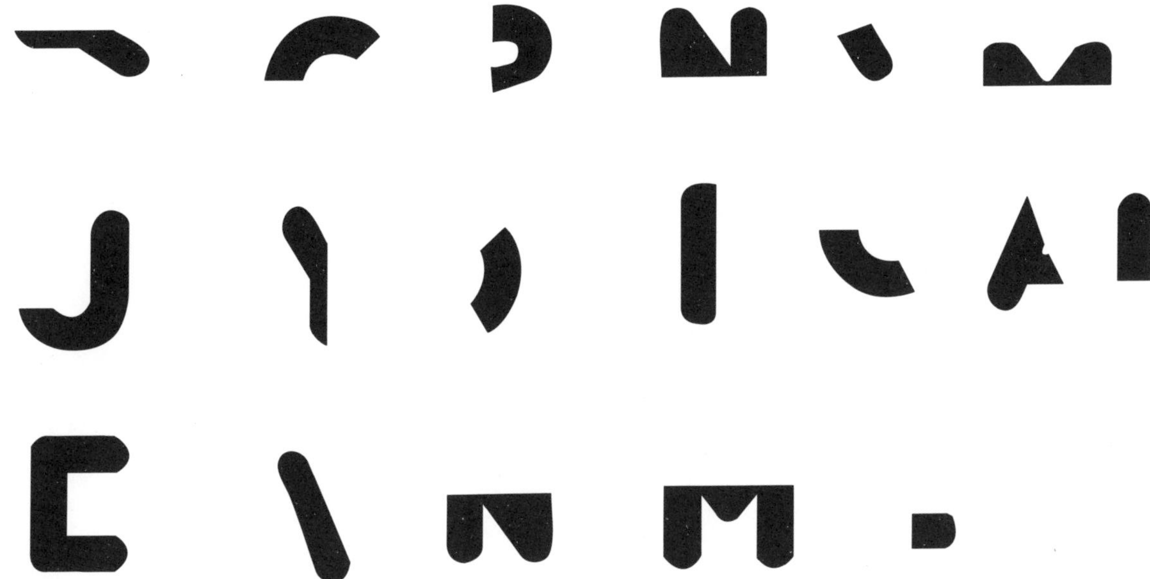

Wise Words

ANALYSIS **CREATIVE THINKING**

Can you determine the next letter in this progression?

A P S I A P __

Answers on page 176.

Bugs in the System

ATTENTION | LANGUAGE | VISUAL SEARCH

Every word listed is contained within this group of letters. The words can be found horizontally, vertically, or diagonally. They may read either backward or forward.

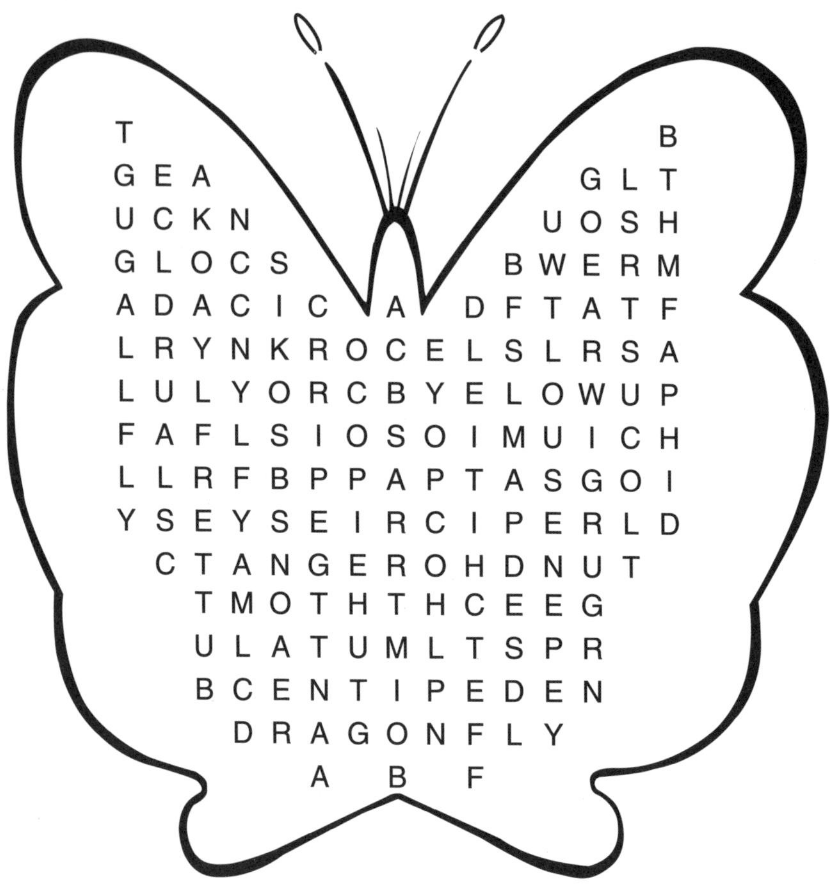

ANT	BUTTERFLY	CRICKET	HORNET	SCORPION
APHID	CATERPILLAR	DRAGONFLY	LOCUST	SPIDER
BEDBUG	CENTIPEDE	EARWIG	LOUSE	THRIPS
BEETLE	CICADA	FLEA	MAYFLY	TSETSE
BLOWFLY	COCKROACH	GALLFLY	MOTH	WASP
		GNAT		

Answers on page 176.

Level 2

ATTENTION | LANGUAGE | GENERAL KNOWLEDGE | VISUAL SEARCH

Find It!, Part I

This is a word search with an added twist. Instead of a list of words to find, we've provided a list of categories. Your challenge is to find 3 items in each category within the box of letters below. The words can be found horizontally, vertically, or diagonally. They may read either backward or forward.

3 gems	3 African animals	3 car makes	3 artists
____________	____________	____________	____________
____________	____________	____________	____________
____________	____________	____________	____________

```
C H S A D Q T W F Z Q
M A F E R R A R I S J
A T D N O M A I D G F
T E A I I L A P O T G
I E L Q L T O Y O T A
S H I W N L F W Y E M
S C V E F F A R I G L
E C R O S S A C I P B
Z L R U B Y T Z Q E T
```

Answers on page 176.

Find It!, Part II

VERBAL MEMORY

(Do not read this until you have read the previous page!)

The "agenda" for the word-search puzzle on page 57 is a verbal-memory workout. How many of these words appeared in the grid? Check them off on this list:

___ LION	___ GIRAFFE	___ RHINO	___ CORVETTE	___ TOYOTA
___ MONET	___ GAZELLE	___ ONYX	___ DIAMOND	___ DA VINCI
___ JAGUAR	___ FERRARI	___ CHEETAH	___ PICASSO	___ OPAL
___ HYENA	___ PEARL	___ FORD	___ RUBY	___ VAN GOGH
___ CADILLAC	___ SAPPHIRE	___ MATISSE		

Anagrams in the Abstract

LANGUAGE

It's easy enough to show a picture of a tambourine or a car, but how do you depict an abstraction, such as "wisdom" or "character"? We think you're up to the task! Unscramble the listed phrases, then put the correct letters and numbers together to make the abstract concrete.

1. APE MYTH
2. MY ROME
3. HOLY HIPPOS!
4. TIRE CAVITY
5. LYRE BIT
6. NO CREAM

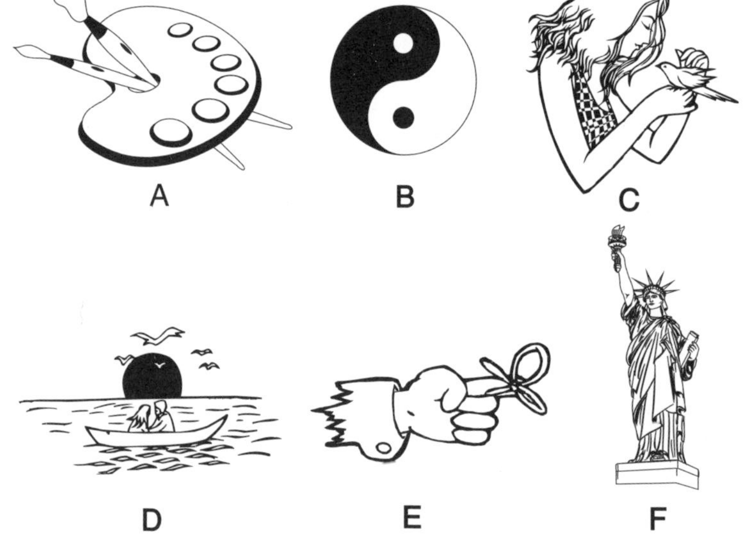

Answers on page 176.

Made Ya Laugh!

LANGUAGE LOGIC

Cryptograms are messages in substitution code. Break the code to read the message. For example, THE SMART CAT might become FVO QWGDF JGF if F is substituted for T, V for H, O for E, and so on. The code is the same for each cryptogram below. Hint: Look for repeated letters. E, T, A, O, N, R, and I are the most often used letters. A single letter is usually A or I; OF, IS, and IT are common 2-letter words; THE and AND are common 3-letter words.

1. "SGO PK MGCO VXBB WM X 'IEWBPWJD?' WM BKKTN BWTC WM'N UWJWNGCP. SGO WNJ'M WM X 'IEWBM?' "

—ACZZO NCWJUCBP

2. X UZCEPWXJ NBWL WN SGCJ OKE NXO KJC MGWJD IEM HCXJ OKEZ HKMGCZ.

3. GCZ YKVXIEBXZO SXN XN IXP XN, BWTC, SGXMCYCZ.

4. "W LBXJMCP NKHC IWZP NCCP. X IWZP DZCS. JKS W PKJ'M TJKS SGXM MK UCCP WM."

—NMCYCJ SZWDGM

5. SGCZC PK UKZCNM ZXJDCZN DK MK DCM XSXO UZKH WM XBB?

Answers on page 176.

Why Can't We Make Just One?

LANGUAGE

Use the 6 letters below to form a common word (not a proper name) that answers the title question—and is also a wryly funny comment on our language.

Why Worry?

LANGUAGE PLANNING

Complete the horizontal phrase by finding the merging phrases.

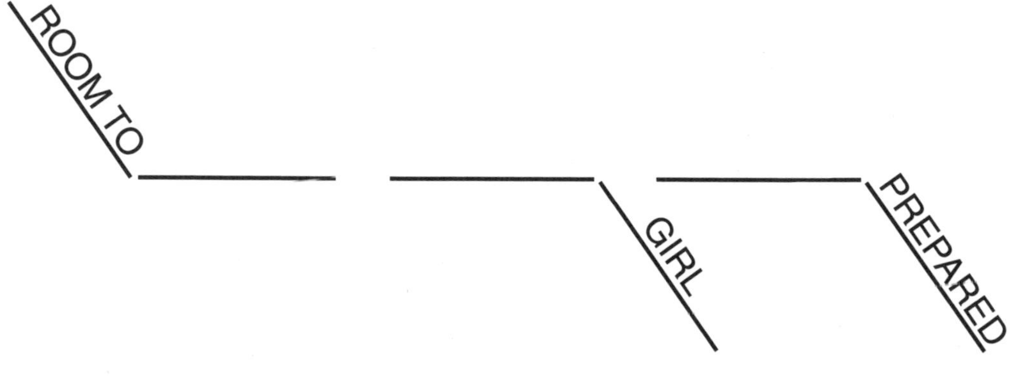

Answers on page 176.

Sudoku

LOGIC

To solve a sudoku puzzle, place the numbers 1 through 9 in some order in each row, column, and 3×3 box. Each puzzle has some numbers filled in—you just need to work out the rest. You'll never have to guess; the puzzle can be solved using only the power of deduction.

1		2				7	9	4
							1	3
		9			4	2		6
	8		1	7				
7			9		3			2
				8	2		3	
8		7	6			3		
3	1							
6	2	5				4		8

Word Jigsaw

SPATIAL PLANNING

Fit the pieces into the frame to form common, uncapitalized words reading across and down crossword-style. There's no need to rotate the pieces; they'll fit as shown, with each piece used exactly once.

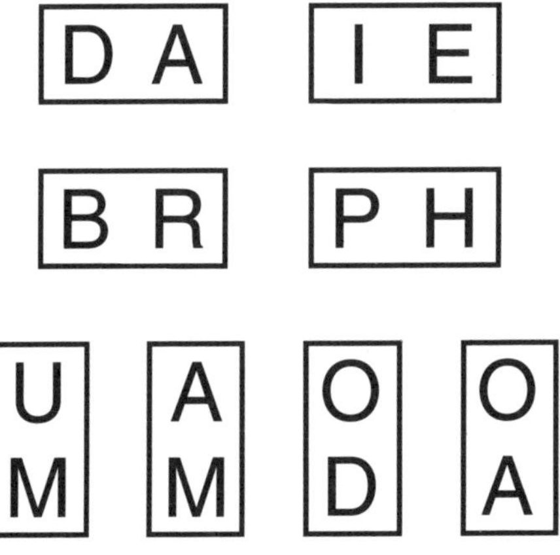

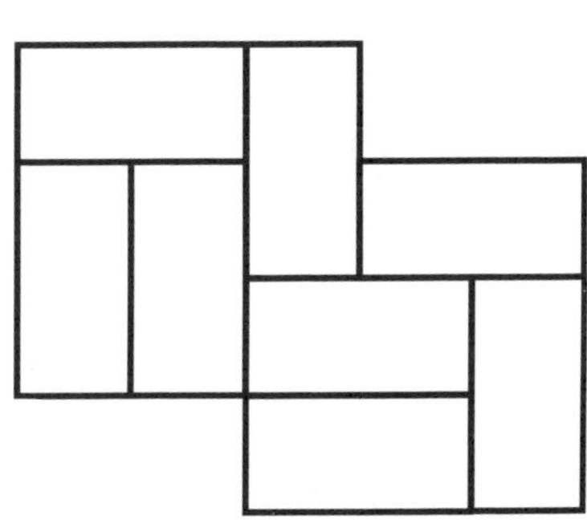

Answers on pages 176–177.

Geometric Shapes

SPATIAL REASONING

Divide the whole grid into smaller geometric shapes by drawing straight lines that follow either the full grid lines or the full diagonals of the square cells. Each formed shape must have exactly one symbol inside, which represents it but might not look identical to it.

Hints: The parallelogram is not inside a rectangle or a square. The trapezoid has two sides parallel, but its other two sides are not parallel.

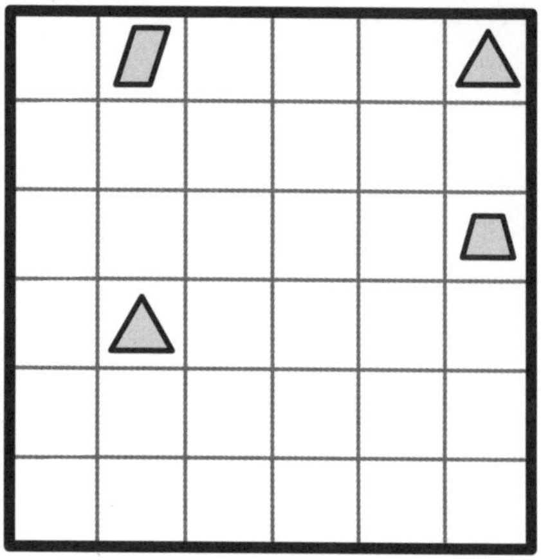

Count the Shapes

ATTENTION

How many squares can you find in the shape below?

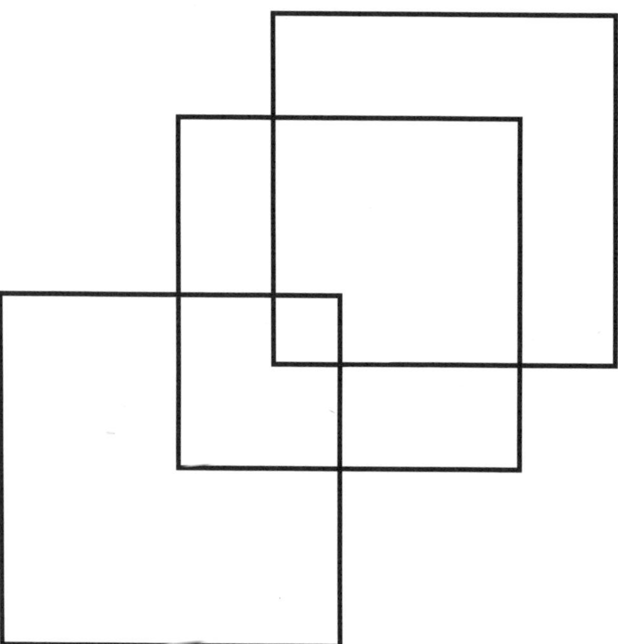

Answers on page 177.

It All Adds Up

COMPUTATION LOGIC

Fill in the empty squares with numbers 1 through 9. The numbers in each row must add up to the totals in the right-hand column. The numbers in each column must add up to the totals on the bottom line. The numbers in each corner-to-corner diagonal must add up to the totals in the upper and lower right corners.

				18
	8	7		**24**
		6	4	**20**
2			3	**16**
1			2	**12**
10	**26**	**22**	**14**	**18**

Totally Cubular!

PLANNING SPATIAL REASONING

Legend has it that the inventor of this cube has a dark side. Not content to produce a puzzle that can be solved only by bright 8-year-olds, he came up with a maze on top of a cube. Can you come to the rescue of the black dot on the top corner of the cube and help him find the shortest route to the gray square in the bottom-right corner?

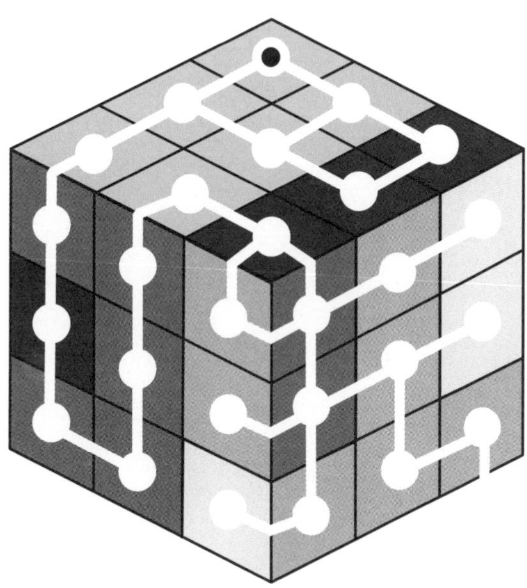

Answers on page 177.

Checkerboard Puzzle

PLANNING SPATIAL REASONING

Moving diagonally, can you find a single, unbroken path from the circle in the upper left corner to the diamond in the lower right? Your path must alternate between circles and diamonds. There's only one way to do it.

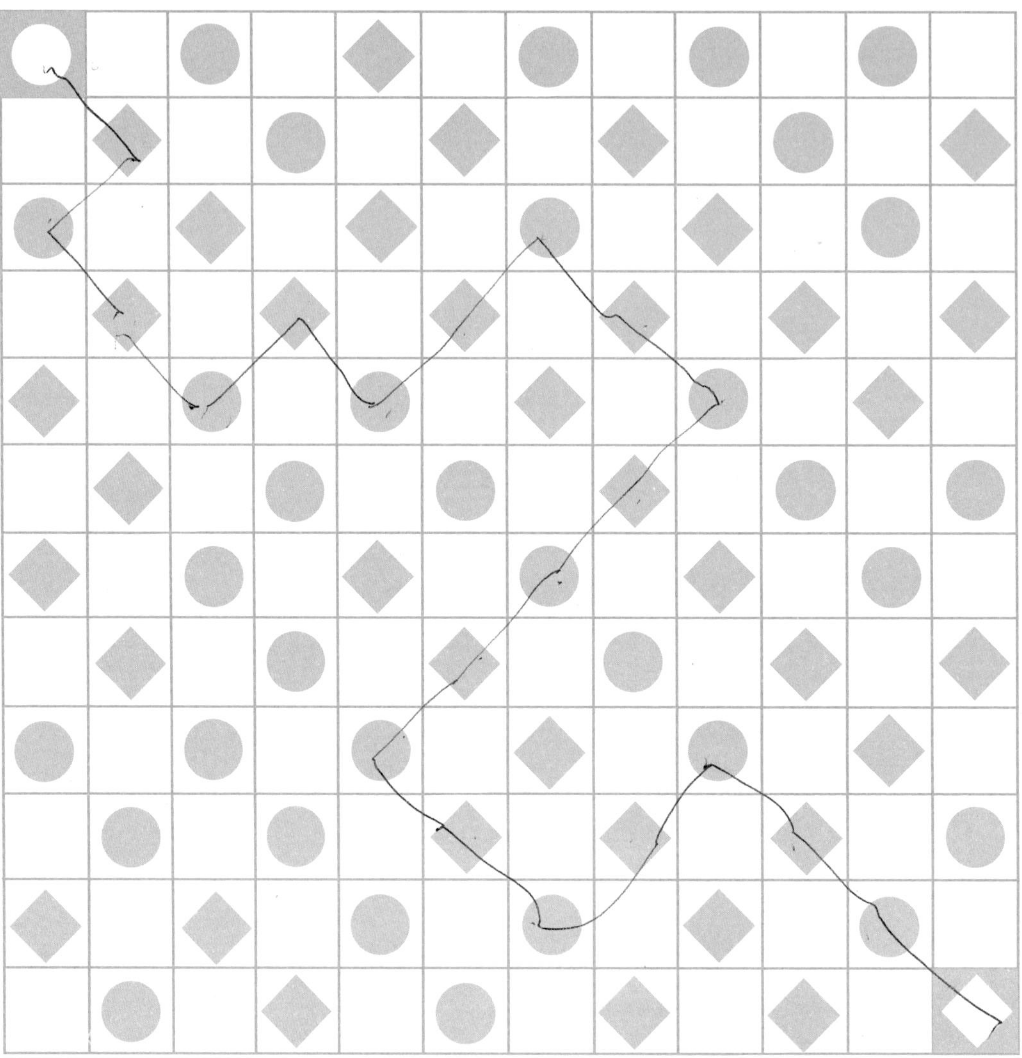

Answer on page 177.

December the What?

LOGIC

You are cordially invited to attend the annual Festival of Games. The contest will be in December, but competition begins the moment you read this invitation. Hope to see you there!

1. The date of the contest is not a multiple of 5.
2. The date is not the eve of a major holiday.
3. Neither of the digits of the date are the same, nor is the second digit equal to one more than the first.
4. The 2-digit date has a sum that is less than 7.
5. The contest is not on a Monday.

DECEMBER

SUN	MON	TUE	WED	THU	FRI	SAT
		1	2	3	4	5
6	7	8	9	10	11	12
13	14	15	16	17	18	19
20	21	22	23	24	25	26
27	28	29	30	31		

Answer on page 177.

Spark Your Mind

Geometric Cube Construction

SPATIAL REASONING

Which one of the cubes can be made from the unfolded sample?

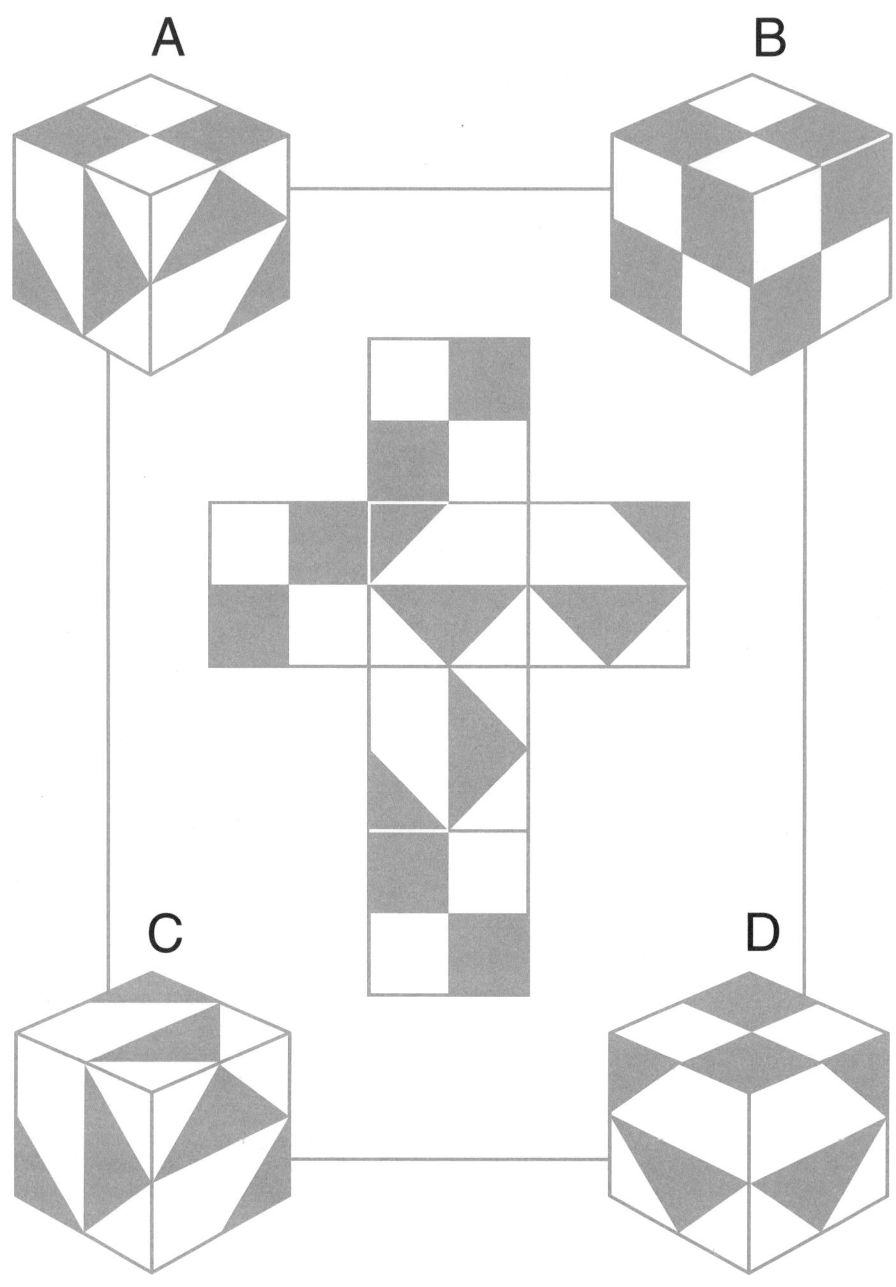

Answer on page 177.

Fitting Words

LANGUAGE LOGIC PLANNING

In this miniature crossword, the clues are listed randomly and are numbered for convenience only. It is up to you to figure out the placement of the 9 answers. To help you out, we've inserted one letter in the grid, and this is the *only* occurrence of that letter in the completed puzzle.

Clues

1. Hindu sage
2. Accustom
3. Over again
4. Abominable snowman
5. Credit's counterpart
6. Disencumbers
7. Tattered and torn
8. Quick haircut
9. Big horn

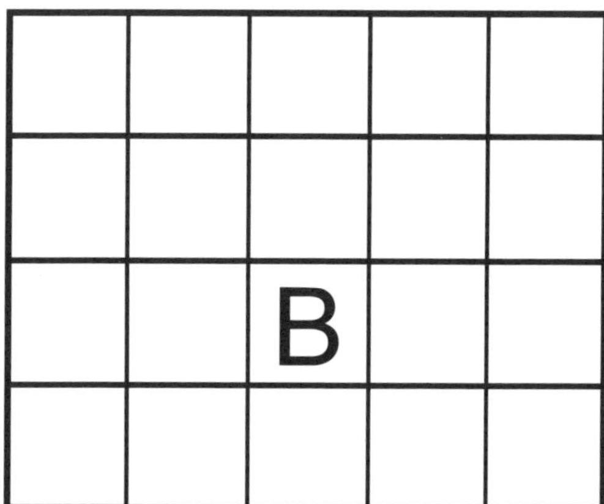

Geometric Shapes

SPATIAL REASONING

Divide the whole grid into smaller geometric shapes by drawing straight lines that follow either the full grid lines or the full diagonals of the square cells. Each formed shape must have exactly one symbol inside, which represents it but might not look identical to it. (In other words, a triangle you draw must have only a triangle symbol within it, although the drawn triangle and the triangle symbol may look slightly different.) Hint: The rectangle symbol cannot be contained in a square.

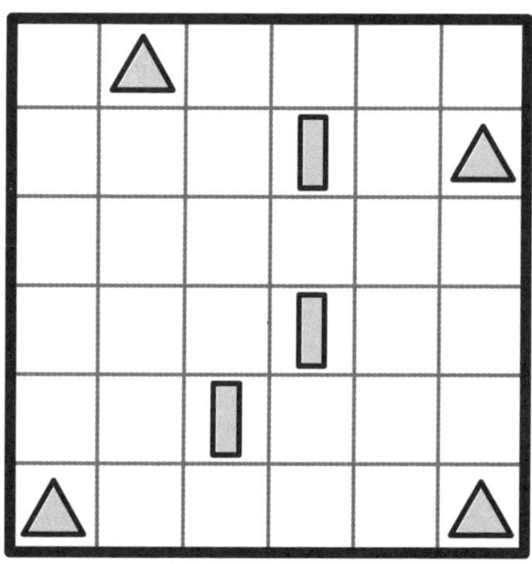

Answers on page 177.

Stop and Smell the Flowers

LANGUAGE LOGIC PLANNING

The letters in the word ROSE can be found in boxes 6, 8, 16, and 23, but not necessarily in that order. Similarly, the letters in all the other flower names can be found in the boxes indicated. Your task is to insert all the letters of the alphabet into the boxes. If you do this correctly, the shaded squares will reveal the names of 2 more flowers.

Hint: Look for names that share a single letter. For example, TULIP shares an L with AZALEA, a P with SNOWDROP, and an I with ORCHID. By comparing the number lists, you can deduce the values of those letters.

AQUILEGIA: 5, 7, 8, 11, 12, 13, 21

AZALEA: 7, 8, 14, 21

BEGONIA: 5, 6, 8, 12, 21, 22, 25

CARNATION: 3, 5, 6, 9, 16, 21, 22

DAFFODIL: 5, 6, 7, 10, 19, 21

HONEYSUCKLE: 3, 6, 7, 8, 13, 18, 22, 23, 24, 26

JASMINE: 2, 5, 8, 17, 21, 22, 23

JONQUIL: 2, 5, 6, 7, 11, 13, 22

ORCHID: 3, 5, 6, 16, 19, 26

OXALIS: 1, 5, 6, 7, 21, 23

OXEYE: 1, 6, 8, 24

ROSE: 6, 8, 16, 23

SNOWDROP: 6, 15, 16, 19, 20, 22, 23

TULIP: 5, 7, 9, 13, 20

VERONICA: 3, 4, 5, 6, 8, 16, 21, 22

ZINNIA: 5, 14, 21, 22

1	2	3	4	5	6	7	8	9	10	11	12	13
14	15	16	17	18	19	20	21	22	23	24	25	26

Answers on page 177.

Batteries Not Included

LANGUAGE

Cryptograms are messages in substitution code. Break the code to read the message. For example, THE SMART CAT might become FVO QWGDF JGF if F is substituted for T, V for H, O for E, and so on. The code is the same for each cryptogram below. Hint: Look for repeated letters. E, T, A, O, N, R, and I are the most often used letters. A single letter is usually A or I; OF, IS, and IT are common 2-letter words; THE and AND are common 3-letter words.

1. VJOT QVVTOSPH NTZCGNTU.

2. CVT JLPH QV UGNTXITU.

3. QV VTTL JL IW.

4. QWJGU XJLIQXI YGIM VEGL.

5. QFFPH JLPH IJ QKKTXITU QNTQ.

6. HJC OCVI ST FNTVTLI IJ YGL.

7. MQNOKCP JN KQIQP GK VYQPPJYTU.

8. LJ FCNXMQVT LTXTVVQNH!

Answers on page 177.

Presidential Puzzle

LOGIC PLANNING SPATIAL REASONING

Can you arrange the names below into the grid? There is only one way to do it.

4 Letters

Ford

5 Letters

Nixon

Tyler

6 Letters

Hoover

Wilson

7 Letters

Clinton

Lincoln

9 Letters

Cleveland

10 Letters

Eisenhower

George Bush

James K. Polk

11 Letters

James Monroe

12 Letters

Ronald Reagan

13 Letters

Ulysses S. Grant

Zachary Taylor

14 Letters

Calvin Coolidge

Warren G. Harding

15 Letters

James Earl Carter

John Quincy Adams

Millard Fillmore

Thomas Jefferson

16 Letters

Benjamin Harrison

George Washington

17 Letters

Chester Alan Arthur

Theodore Roosevelt

William Howard Taft

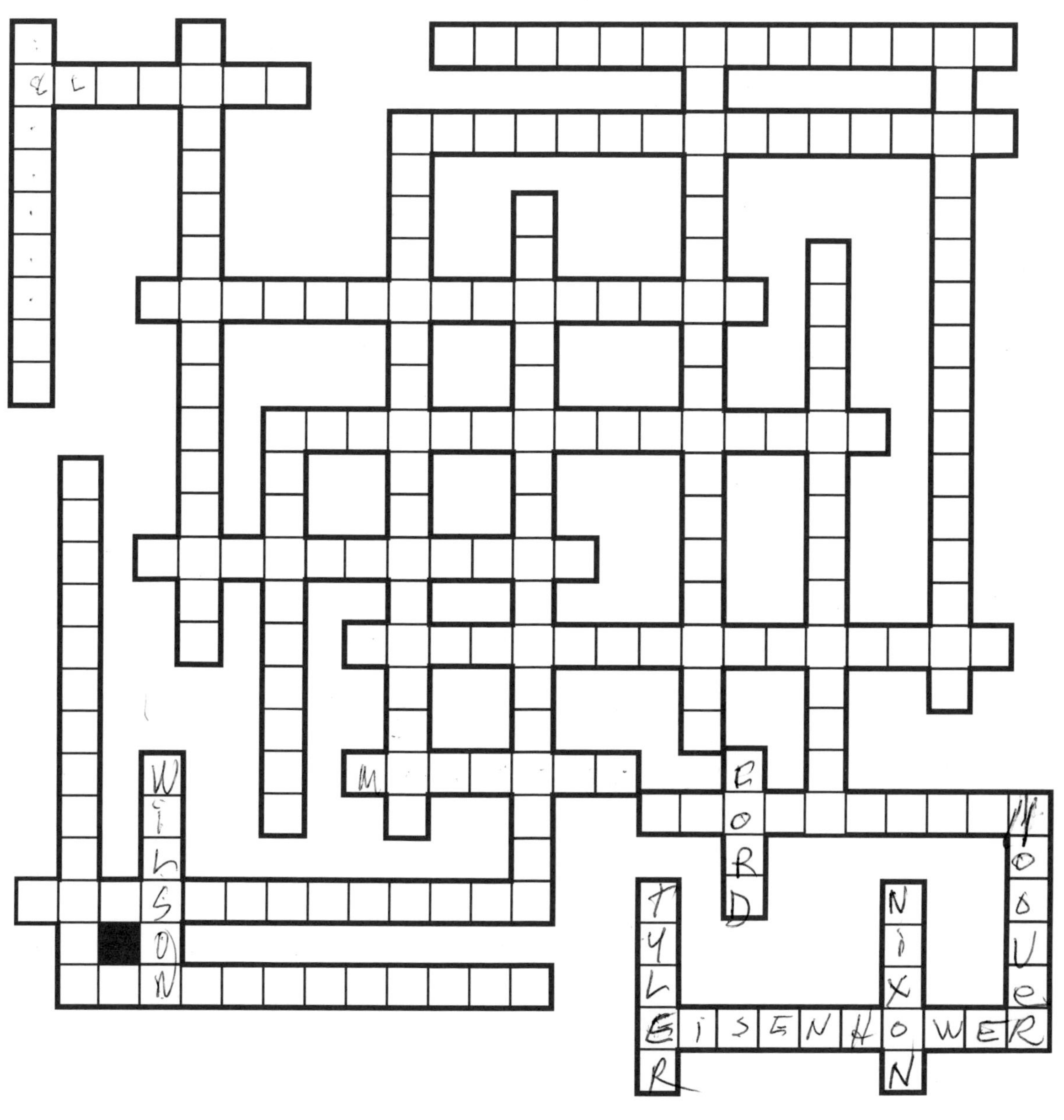

Answers on page 178.

Circle Takes the Square

PLANNING

SPATIAL REASONING

All you have to do to solve this puzzle is move in a single, unbroken path from the circle in the upper left corner to the circle in the lower right. Your path must alternate between circles and squares, and you can only move horizontally and vertically (not diagonally).

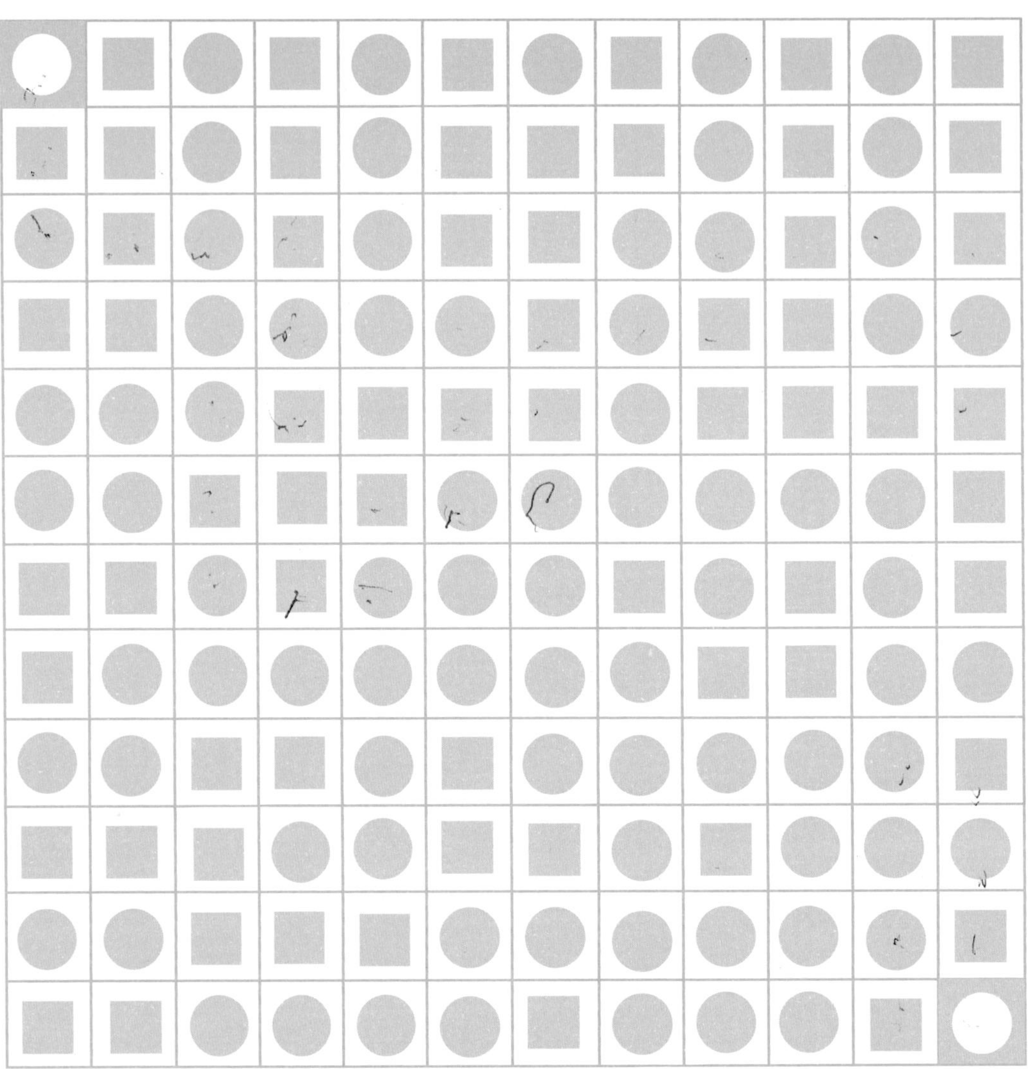

Answer on page 178.

Barbershop Duet

ATTENTION

Something has gone drastically wrong in this barbershop. We count 7 wrong things. Can you find them all?

Word of Mouth

LOGIC PLANNING SPATIAL REASONING

Fill each square with one of the 5 letters of the word MOUTH so that each row, each column, and both diagonals contain all 5 letters exactly once. We've inserted 6 letters to get you started.

T		H		M
	T			
			M	
U				

Answers on page 178.

Road Trip!

PLANNING

SPATIAL REASONING

This confused driver is having trouble finding the gas station—and he's running on empty! Follow the arrows to help him find the correct route.

Answer on page 178.

Level 2

Famished Family

PLANNING

SPATIAL REASONING

How fast can mom get dinner on the table?

Answer on page 178.

FAN THE FLAMES

LEVEL 3

Multiplication Table

COMPUTATION LOGIC

Enter the digits 1 to 5 into the grid so that each row and column contains each digit just once. The number on each circle gives the product of the 4 digits surrounding it.

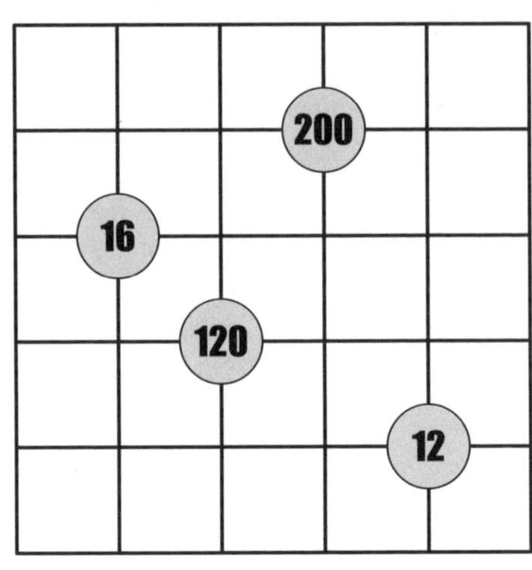

Dissection

SPATIAL REASONING

Cut the figure into 2 equal parts following the grid lines. The parts should be the same in size and shape but they may be rotated and/or turned over.

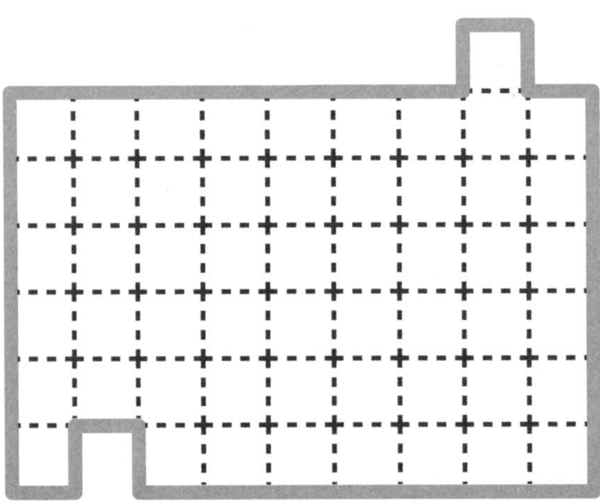

Answers on page 178.

Not-So-Happy Birthday

LOGIC

Molly had heard that "40 is the new 30," but she didn't believe it and wanted to stay in her 30s for a while longer. As usual, when her husband Homer tried to understand it, he instead stuck his foot in his mouth and said something that made it worse. After doing the math on a piece of paper, Homer said to Molly: "The day before yesterday, you were 39 years old. But next year, you will be 42." Molly realized he was right but hit him with a pillow anyway. How did Molly not only leave her 30s, but skip a couple of years in the process, too?

Finding a Digit

ATTENTION **VISUAL SEARCH**

In the grid, find a stylized digit *exactly* like the one shown next to the grid. The digit can be rotated but not mirrored.

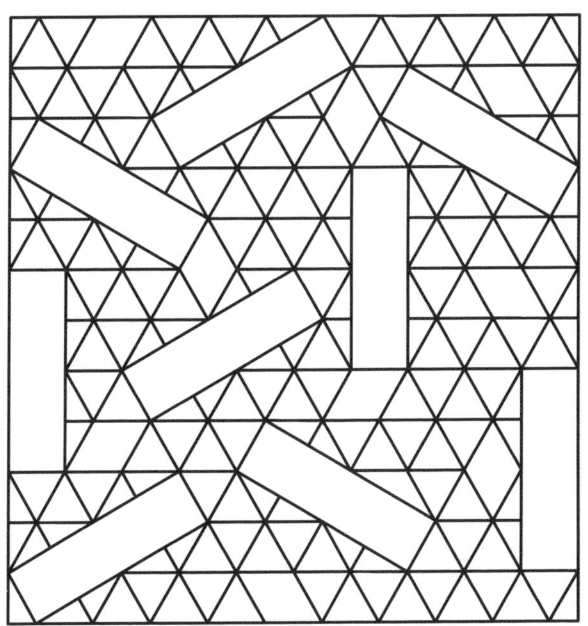

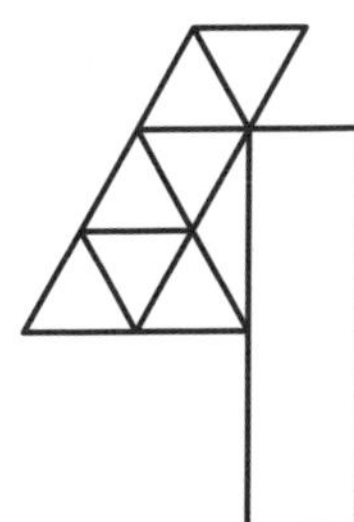

Answers on page 179.

Word Columns

LOGIC PLANNING SPATIAL REASONING

Find the hidden phrase by using the letters directly below each of the blank squares. Each letter is used only once.

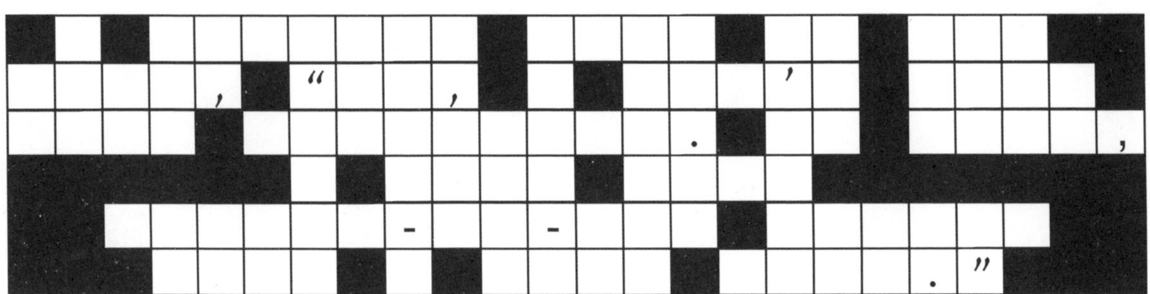

													s									
			h			b		I			I		d			r	o					
			t		h	e	a	l	t	i	v	k	y	d		b	e		h	a	r	
	i	m	e	h	a	I	l	n	d	n	s	l	a	w	m	t	n		h	i	t	
w	o	f	r	t	s	e	N	a	i	l	i	a	i	o	n	I	n	e	t	a	c	e
y	A	u	o	u	r	n	r	o	i	k	e	e	e	o	u	i	t	t	f	e	s	t

Brain-Friendly Foods

Fruits and vegetables provide antioxidants that help protect the brain and maintain memory function. Blueberries and strawberries are especially good sources!

Answer on page 179.

Level 3

SPATIAL REASONING

Another Doggone Jigsaw

These shapes, when pieced together properly, will reveal a nice silhouette of human's best friend. But the pieces haven't been flipped, rotated, or otherwise changed—all you have to do is fit 'em together (using just your eyes) to get an appreciative "Arf!"

Answer on page 179.

The Logic of Crayons

LOGIC

Sabrina, Jill, Kelly, and Kris are 4 teen girls. (Despite their names, they have no known relation to Charlie's Angels.) The girls like to get together occasionally for a "color therapy" session, which consists of gossip, pizza, comparing lip gloss, and coloring with crayons. They especially love the jazzy names that Creative Colors has come up with for some of their crayons. The girls also like to check out the latest lip glosses.

One of the girls loves the crayon color Neon Carrot. Another adores Vivid Tangerine. One can't resist Tickle Me Pink, and the fourth one can't wait to try to color inside the lines with Mauvelous.

Their lip-gloss flavors are Strawberry Smackers, Hard Candy Lollipop, Bubble Gum, and Plum Wicked.

Using the clues below, see if you can figure out each girl's crayon color and lip-gloss flavor. Here are your clues:

1. Sabrina is a health-food nut (no pizza, thanks), so she likes crayons and lip-gloss flavors that remind her of fruits and vegetables.
2. Kelly borrowed the Vivid Tangerine crayon one day from one of the other girls. She also felt like borrowing the Bubble Gum lip gloss just once.
3. Jill tends to favor anything that reminds her of her doll Elmo, so she picked a crayon that did.
4. Kris is trying to cultivate a pouty, seductive look, so she picked a lip gloss that sounded promising and just a bit devilish—in a totally wholesome way, of course. She also likes fruity flavors.
5. Kelly likes to color with various shades of violets and purples, especially when they sound "wunnerful"!

6. One of Kris's favorite crayon colors is pink, but someone else had already chosen that color.

7. Kris is not a big fan of vegetables, but she does like fruits.

8. The girl who likes violet shades also likes suckers—the "all-day" candy kind, that is.

9. Sabrina has always been partial to the only fruit that has its seeds on the outside, so she chose that for her lip gloss.

Girl	Crayon Color	Lip Gloss
Sabrina		
Jill		
Kelly		
Kris		

Answers on page 179.

Sage Advice

ANALYSIS | CREATIVE THINKING

Can you determine the next letter in this progression?

A F A H M A S ___

Let's Make Bread!

LANGUAGE | PLANNING

Change just one letter on each line to go from the top word to the bottom word. Do not change the order of the letters. You must put a common English word at each step.

FLOUR

____

____

____

____

____

BREAD

Answers on page 179.

Say It Again, Sam

LANGUAGE

Homophones are words that sound the same but are spelled differently. Solve each clue below with a pair of homophones. For example, "a breezy eagle's nest" is an "airy aerie."

1. Consumed ⅔ of a dozen: ________
2. Insert commercial: ________
3. Whitish bucket: ________
4. Composition on tranquility: ________
5. Twin fruit: ________
6. Jurist on a wharf: ________
7. Unadorned aircraft: ________
8. Entire cavity: ________
9. Completely sacred: ________
10. Henry Clay or Daniel Webster's toupee: ________
11. Somebody was victorious: ________
12. Sea animal's groan: ________
13. Egotistical blood vessel: ________
14. A pull with a certain digit: ________
15. Compose correctly: ________
16. Sardonic grain: ________
17. Only spirit: ________
18. A contract stowed in a suitcase: ________
19. A seer's bottom line: ________
20. High-ranking maize unit: ________
21. Healthy storm ice: ________
22. Grief before noon: ________
23. Assembled hot dog condiment: ________
24. That extra piece of flattery that finished the praise: ________
25. Cotillion cry: ________
26. The agreement to climb: ________

Answers on page 179.

Fan the Flames

Mirror, Mirror

SPATIAL VISUALIZATION

There's no trick here, only a challenge: Draw the mirror image of each of these familiar objects. You may find it harder than you think!

Sudoku

LOGIC

To solve a sudoku puzzle, place the numbers 1 through 9 only once in each row, column, and 3×3 box. Each puzzle has some numbers filled in—you just need to work out the rest. You'll never have to guess; all the puzzles can be solved using the power of deduction.

				7			8	
		8	1		3	7		2
	9					1		
	4	1	8			2		
	7			6			4	
		2			1	9	5	
		7					1	
4		9	7		5	3		
	1			2				

Count the Shapes

ATTENTION

How many squares can you count in the figure below?

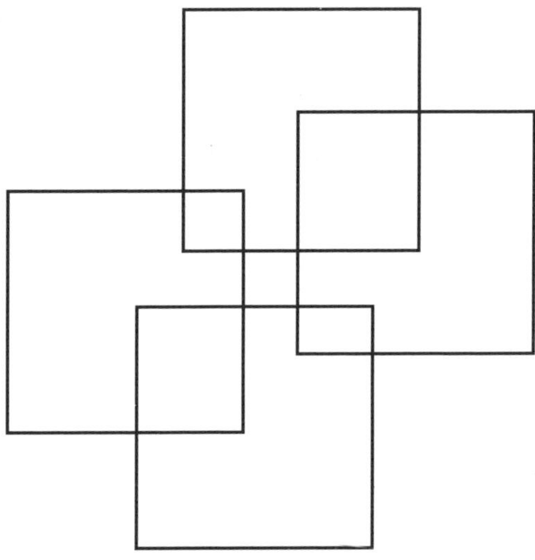

Answers on page 180.

Layer by Layer

CREATIVE THINKING | SPATIAL REASONING

Eighteen sheets of paper—all of them equal in size and shape—were piled on the table. Number the sheets from top to bottom.

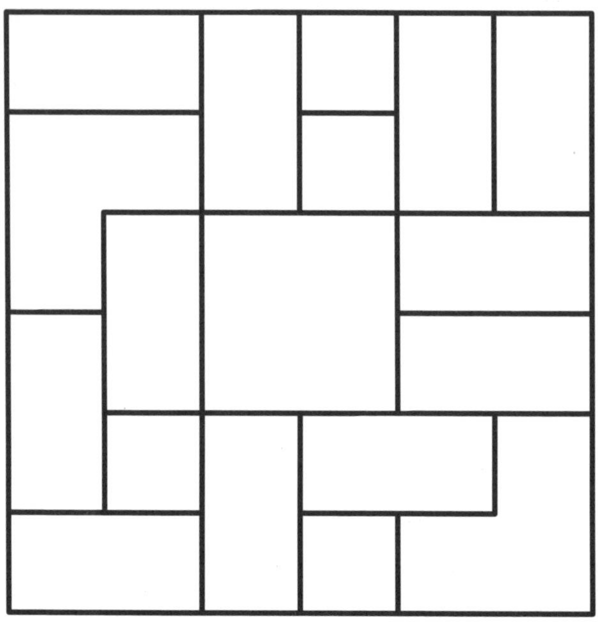

Next Letter?

ANALYSIS | CREATIVE THINKING

What will be the next letter in this progression?

O, T, T, F, F, S, S, _____

Answers on page 180.

Imbroglio of I's

ATTENTION VISUAL SEARCH

This picture contains an imbroglio of things beginning with the letter **I.** We count 13. How many can you find?

Misleading Sequence

CREATIVE THINKING LOGIC

In the progression below, circle 2 numbers that equal 18 when added together.

1 2 3 4 5 6 7 8 9

Answers on page 180.

To the Letter

COMPUTATION CREATIVE THINKING

Each letter represents a different number between 1 and 7. No zeros are used. Can you determine the set of letter values that will make all the equations work? Hints: Start by listing all the combinations of 3 different digits that add up to 9. One of the numbers between 1 and 7 will not be used.

$$A + B + C = 9$$

$$B + D + E = 11$$

$$A + B + B = 13$$

$$E + E + F = 15$$

Name Game

ATTENTION VISUAL SEARCH

Within this grid, you'll find 4 names: 2 men's and 2 women's. The blanks next to each picture indicate how many letters are in each of their names. Reading from left to right, right to left, top to bottom, bottom to top, and all 4 ways diagonally, can you find the number of times each name appears? The grand total for all 4 names is 36.

We filled in a name to get you started.

Answers on page 180.

Logical Hats

COMPUTATION LOGIC

Each of 3 logicians A, B, and C wears a hat with a positive whole number on it. The number on 1 hat is the sum of the numbers on the other 2. Each logician can see the numbers on the other 2 hats but not the number on their own. They have this information and are asked in turn to identify their own number.

A: "I don't know my number."

B: "My number is 15."

What numbers are on A and C?

Fitting Words

LANGUAGE LOGIC PLANNING

In this miniature crossword, the clues are listed randomly and are numbered for convenience only. It is up to you to figure out the placement of the 9 answers. To help you out, we've already inserted one letter in the grid, and this is the *only* occurrence of that letter in the completed puzzle.

Clues

1. "Quiet!"
2. Heavy books
3. Domino on the piano
4. "Goodbye, Pierre!"
5. Golf supporters
6. Screen star
7. Foul matter
8. Spill clumsily
9. Prom ride

				U

Answers on page 180.

Find It

ATTENTION | GENERAL KNOWLEDGE | LANGUAGE | VISUAL SEARCH

This is a word search with an added twist. Instead of a list of words to find, we've provided a list of categories. Your challenge is to find items in each category within the box of letters on the next page. The words can be found in a straight line horizontally, vertically, or diagonally. They may read either backward or forward.

3 Great Lakes

____

____

____

2 musical instruments

____

____

3 colors

____

____

____

2 one-word movie titles

____

____

4 dog breeds

____

____

____

____

2 famous Bobs

____

____

B	O	X	E	R	O	C	H	F	N
L	N	T	G	L	I	O	P	H	E
U	T	N	N	N	P	I	U	L	I
E	A	D	A	E	A	R	G	G	L
G	R	T	R	N	O	A	U	F	L
U	I	I	O	N	E	B	S	P	O
T	O	R	E	B	T	Z	O	D	C
B	D	Y	L	A	N	S	W	A	J

Trivia on the Brain

If you continue to learn and challenge yourself throughout your life, your brain will continue to grow, literally. An active brain produces new dendrites, the "branches" that extend from each nerve cell toward other nerve cells. Dendrites enable nerve cells to communicate with one another in the process of storing and retrieving information.

Answers on page 180.

Easy as ABC

LOGIC

Each row and column contains A, B, C, D, and 2 blank squares. Each letter-and-number indicator refers to the first or second of the 4 letters encountered when traveling inward. Can you complete the grid?

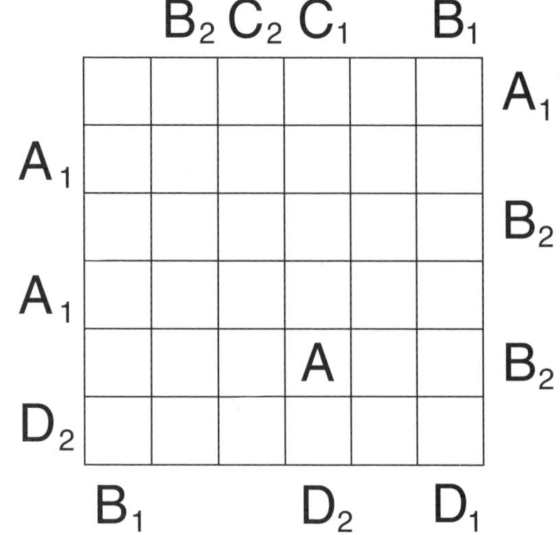

	B_2	C_2	C_1		B_1	
						A_1
A_1						
						B_2
A_1						
			A			B_2
D_2						
B_1			D_2		D_1	

Relying on Hope

LANGUAGE PLANNING

Complete the horizontal phrase by finding the merging phrases.

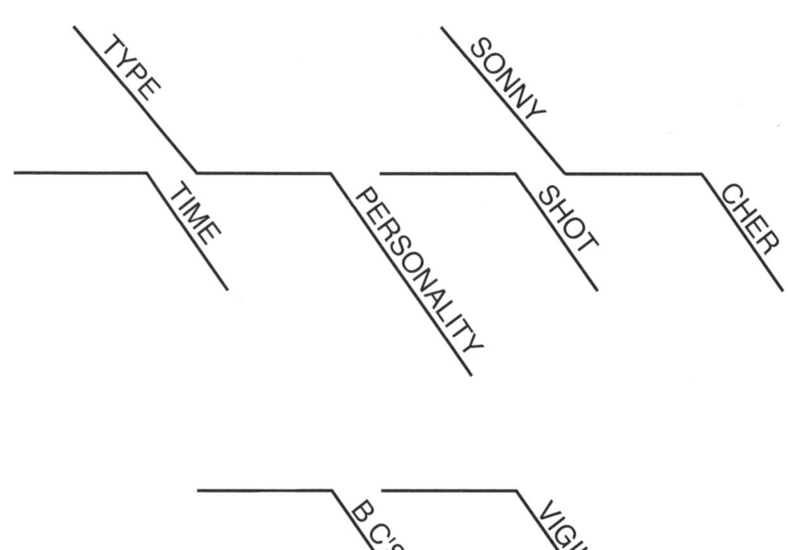

Answers on page 180.

Number Crossword

COMPUTATION **LOGIC**

Use the clues to determine which of the digits 1 through 9 belongs in each square in the diagram. Digits may be repeated within a number, and no zeros are used.

Across

1. A prime number
3. Consecutive even digits, in some order
6. Five times 2-Down
7. A multiple of 13

Down

1. A multiple of 9
2. Consecutive digits, ascending
4. A palindrome
5. Consecutive digits, ascending

1	2		
3		4	5
6			
		7	

The Brain *vs.* The Computer: Similarities and Differences

- Both use electrical signals. Even though electrical signals travel at high speeds in the nervous system, they travel even faster through the wires in a computer.
- Both have a memory that can grow. Computer memory grows by adding computer chips. The brain's memory stores grow through the building of more and stronger synaptic connections.
- Both can change and be modified. The brain is always changing and being modified. There is no "off" for the brain—even when an animal is sleeping, its brain is still active and working. The computer only changes when new hardware or software is added or something is saved in memory. There *is* an "off" for a computer. When the power to a computer is turned off, signals are not transmitted.

Answers on page 181.

Unbearable Jigsaw

SPATIAL REASONING

It's the national animal of Finland and the official animal of 5 U.S. states, and the adjective for it is *ursine*. These shapes, when fitted together properly, will give you its silhouette. The pieces haven't been flipped, rotated, or otherwise changed—all you have to do is fit them together with your eyes.

Answer on page 181.

Count the Shapes

ATTENTION

How many squares do you count in the figure below?

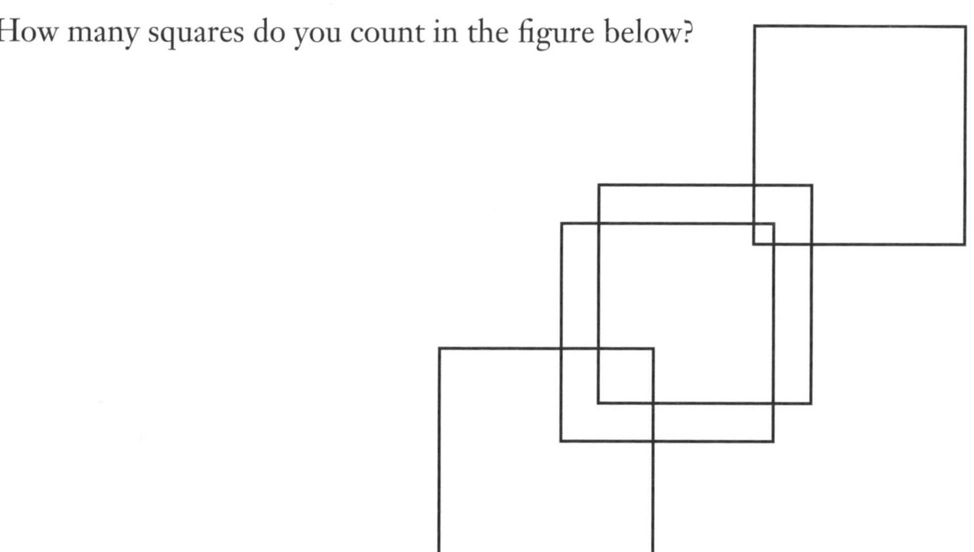

Word Jigsaw

SPATIAL PLANNING

Fit the pieces into the frame to form common, uncapitalized words reading across and down crossword-style. There's no need to rotate the pieces; they'll fit as shown, with each piece used exactly once.

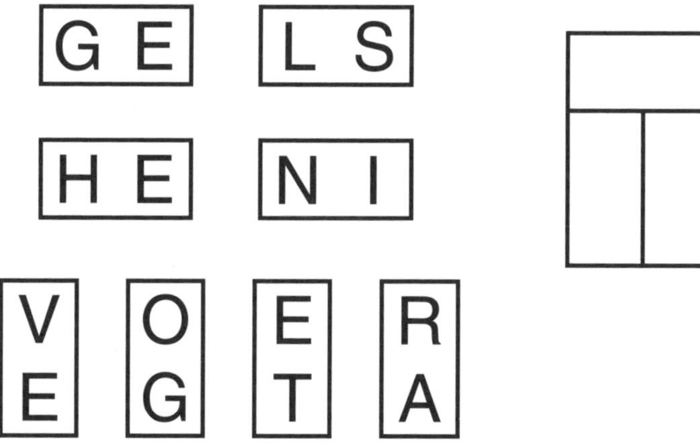

Answers on page 181.

Fit It!

LOGIC | PLANNING | SPATIAL REASONING

Write each word listed on pages 96 and 97 in the grid on the next page. They only fit in the grid one way.

3 Letters

ADA

ASP

MAT

OPT

PGA

SAM

STY

TEA

ZIP

4 Letters

ASHE

EDIE

ERIN

ERNE

ERNO

HAMM

HERA

MOON

MUIR

RIFE

SEAM

SEER

SKIN

SLAG

STOP

TELL

TONY

UNIT

XENA

X OUT

5 Letters

AGAIN

INEPT

IT'S OK

KATIE

MANNA

MATZO

NEGEV

SATES

SCREW

SEWER

SIXTH

SPIKE

TASTE

UNHIP

Level 3

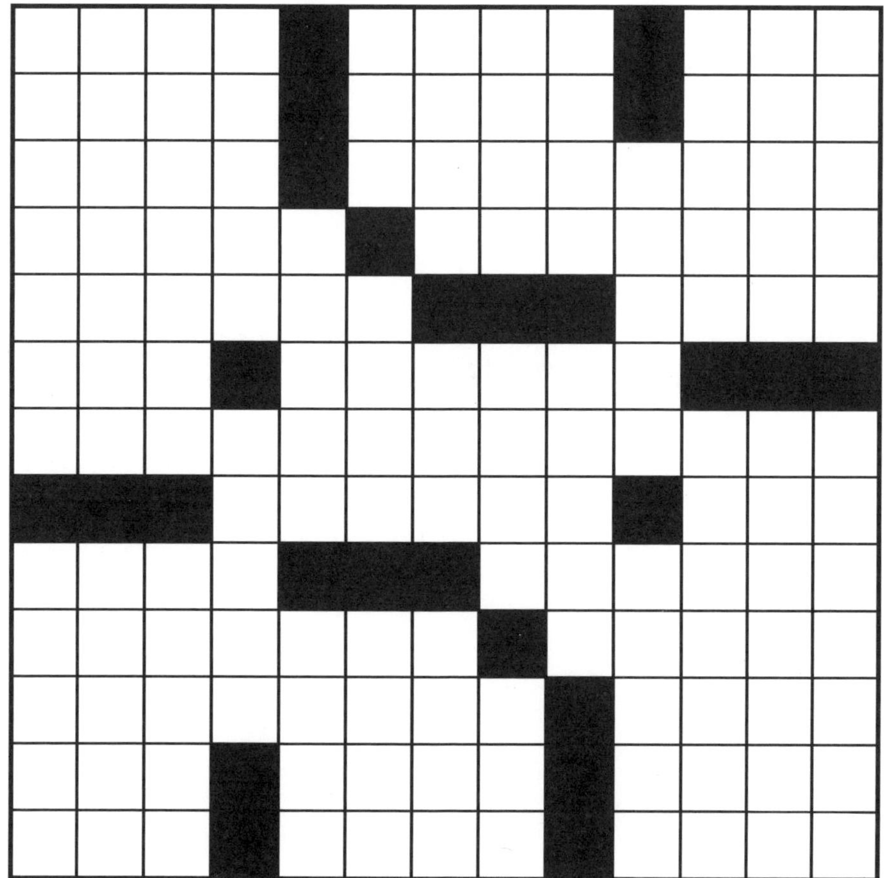

6 Letters

CREAMS

I NEVER

MOTIVE

WITH IT

7 Letters

ANNEXES

EMITTED

MANIKIN

MESSIAH

ON A TEAR

ORLANDO

RAVIOLI

STEEPLE

8 Letters

PARISIAN

THE WORKS

13 Letters

HORSEFEATHERS

Answers on page 181.

Number Maze

COMPUTATION SPATIAL REASONING

Each number you land on in this maze tells you how many squares away either vertically or horizontally your next move must be. You may not move diagonally. For example, your first move from the 4 in the upper left corner must be either 4 squares vertically (to the 2) or 4 squares horizontally (to the 3). If you land on a square with a zero, you've reached a dead end and will need to backtrack. There's only one way to reach the star.

4	5	3	2	3
4	2	5	4	2
1	0	2	2	3
0	3	2	3	3
2	3	1	4	4
2	0	4	1	★

Why Walk When You Can Ride?

LANGUAGE PLANNING

Change just one letter on each line to go from the top word to the bottom word. Do not change the order of the letters. You must put a common English word at each step.

WALK

______

______

______

RIDE

Answers on page 181.

Anagrammatically Correct

LANGUAGE

Fill in the blanks in each sentence below with 4-letter words that are anagrams (rearrangements of the same letters) of one another.

1. Use _______ baseball bat if you want to get more _______.
2. Male cats are called _______ by _______ people.
3. Unfortunately, the man _______ his _______ hat on the bus.
4. The old man related his _______ until _______ in the evening.
5. An _______ of land was the prize promised to the winner of the _______.
6. My finger is still _____ where I pricked it on the thorn of a _____.
7. It rained _______ and dogs on the _______ during the last two _______ of the play when it was performed in the park.
8. It was a _______ to clean the pots and _______ while the kids were taking their _______.

Pyramid

GENERAL KNOWLEDGE

LANGUAGE

Build this pyramid from top to bottom. Start by filling in the answer to the first definition. Find the answer to the next definition by adding a letter to the previous answer and rearaanging the letters; then write it in. Repeat for each level of the pyramid.

1. East: abbr. __
2. Olivia ____ Havilland __ __
3. Lair __ __ __
4. Tear apart __ __ __ __
5. Beneath __ __ __ __ __
6. Put up with __ __ __ __ __ __
7. Set of false teeth __ __ __ __ __ __ __
8. Made a daring attempt __ __ __ __ __ __ __ __
9. Exciting experience __ __ __ __ __ __ __ __ __
10. Not visited by tourists __ __ __ __ __ __ __ __ __ __

Answers on page 181.

Fan the Flames

All That & Less

ATTENTION | LANGUAGE | VISUAL SEARCH

Find each of the listed words and phrases diagonally in this grid (but always in a straight line). When you've discovered them all, the leftover letters will spell something that we're sure you've already noticed.

ABANDON SHIP
BRANDY ALEXANDER
CANDID CAMERA
CANDLE IN THE WIND
COLONEL SANDERS
CONAN DOYLE
DICK VAN DYKE
DIXIELAND BAND
EYE CANDY
FAN DANCE
GRANDSTAND
HANDEL'S MESSIAH
HAND-TO-HAND COMBAT
INDIRA GANDHI
JIM DANDY
KING FERDINAND
NO CAN DO
ONE-ARMED BANDIT
SAND CASTLES
TAKE A GANDER
THOUSAND ISLANDS

```
T O H E C O Y A E Y I N K S E C
N U N T I & V L B H & I E L E T
T O E E D R Y & & & N C C R S S
H A C M A O E G B G O & E R N H
D & I & & R A & F & L N E Y A H
R J T N O R M E G E L & S I E S
A E O O I C R E I A S E S H & V
E C & D H D & N D L E S I L I S
E K N X I & T I E B E K S X & P
B I Y N E H C N D M & I A C I E
E & & & E L O O S C & I A T F D
N R T W V L A L M S A S T & E P
L A I S O K E Y U B T M A C E D
B N Y C & & C O & L A N E T H E
D A M P H R H I E R C T E R R S
A N D S Y T G S D E B M B O A L
```

Leftover letters spell:______________________________

Answers on page 181.

Level 3

Sign of the Times

COMPUTATION LOGIC

Fill each square of the grid with a number from 1 through 9. The numbers in each row, when multiplied, should produce the total in the right-hand column. The numbers in each column, when multiplied, should produce the total on the bottom line. Important: The number 1 can only be used once in any row or column; other numbers can be repeated.

Hint: Some of the squares contain 5s or 7s. Identify these first.

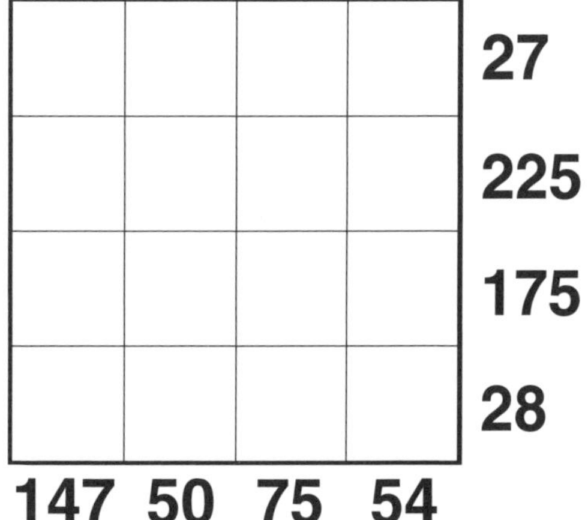

Number Maze

COMPUTATION PLANNING

Find your way through the maze. Start with the 7 in the upper left corner and finish with the 8 in the lower right corner. Move only through spaces containing numbers that are multiples of either 7 or 8.

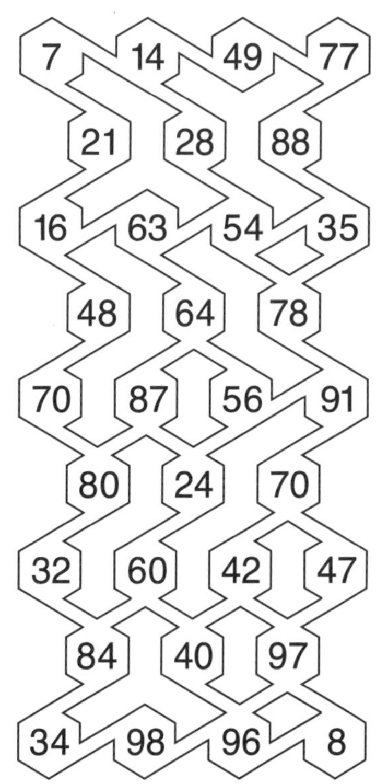

Answers on pages 181–182.

Word Jigsaw

SPATIAL PLANNING

Fit the pieces into the frame to form common, uncapitalized words reading across and down crossword-style. There's no need to rotate the pieces; they'll fit as shown, with each piece used exactly once.

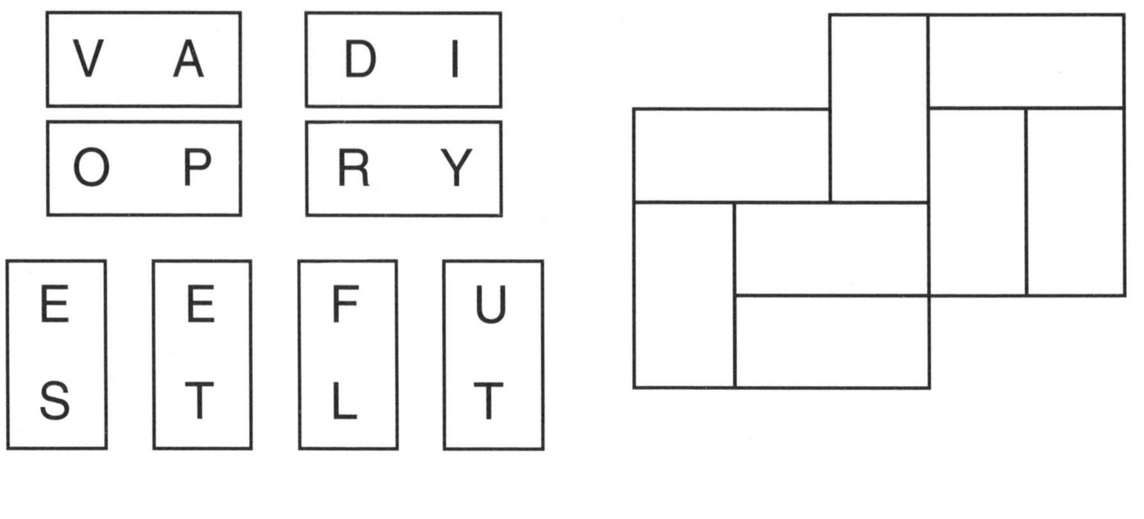

Ageless Logic

COMPUTATION LOGIC

Not wanting to be embarrassed by revealing her age on her birthday, Grandma instead told the grandkids that if they multiplied her age in 5 years by 5, then multiplied her age in 6 years by 6, and added the 2 totals together, they would get a number that is exactly 12 times her current age. When she saw the mighty blaze atop her birthday cake, though, Grandma knew they had figured it out. How old is she?

Answers on page 182.

On the Plus Side

COMPUTATION LOGIC

Fill in the empty squares with numbers 1 through 9. The numbers in each row must add up to the totals in the right-hand column. The numbers in each column must add up to the totals on the bottom line. The numbers in each corner-to-corner diagonal must add up to the totals in the upper and lower right corners.

							26
2	3		8		3	5	34
3		3	9	1		7	31
	2	7		3	6	8	39
9		2	6	7	3		42
1	3		9		2	1	22
3	5	4	7		8		34
2	4	9			2	4	34
28	27	32	49	32	28	40	36

Answers on page 182.

Star Power

LOGIC

Fill the empty squares in the grid so that every starred square is surrounded by digits 1 through 8 with no repeats.

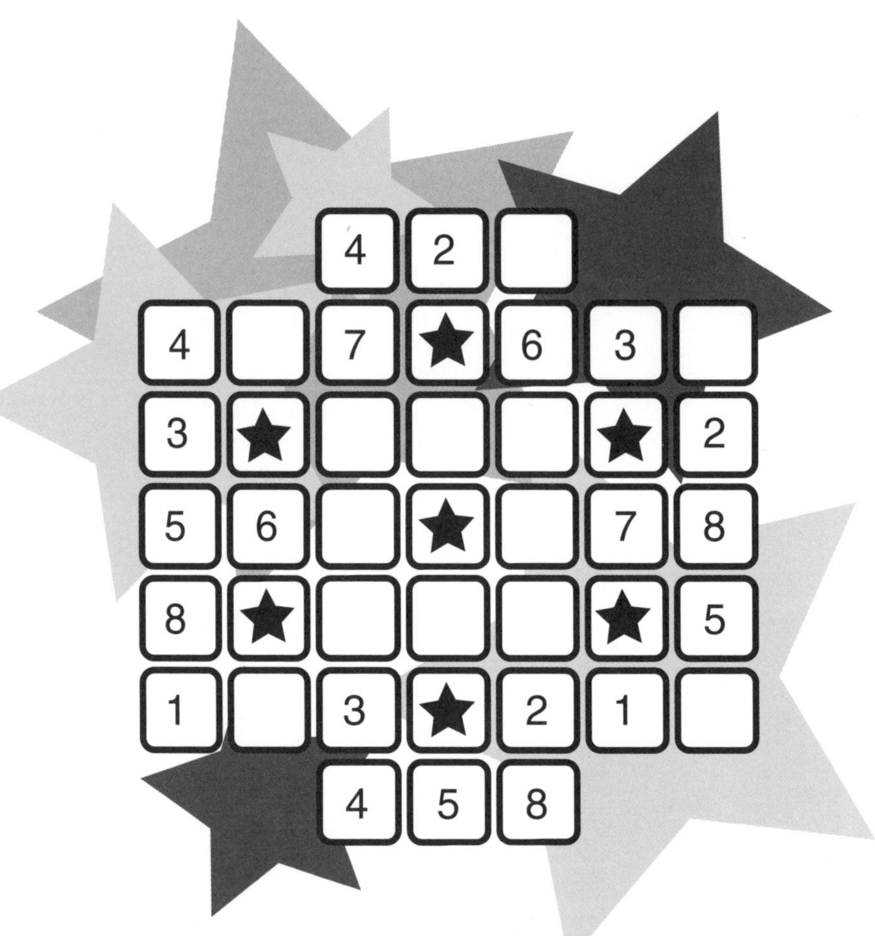

Answer on page 182.

Level 3

SPATIAL VISUALIZATION

Mirror, Mirror

There's no trick here, only a challenge: Draw the mirror image of each of these familiar objects. You may find it harder than you think!

The Office

PLANNING | SPATIAL REASONING

Five minutes left on his break and now he's thirsty! Get him to the water cooler before his break is over!

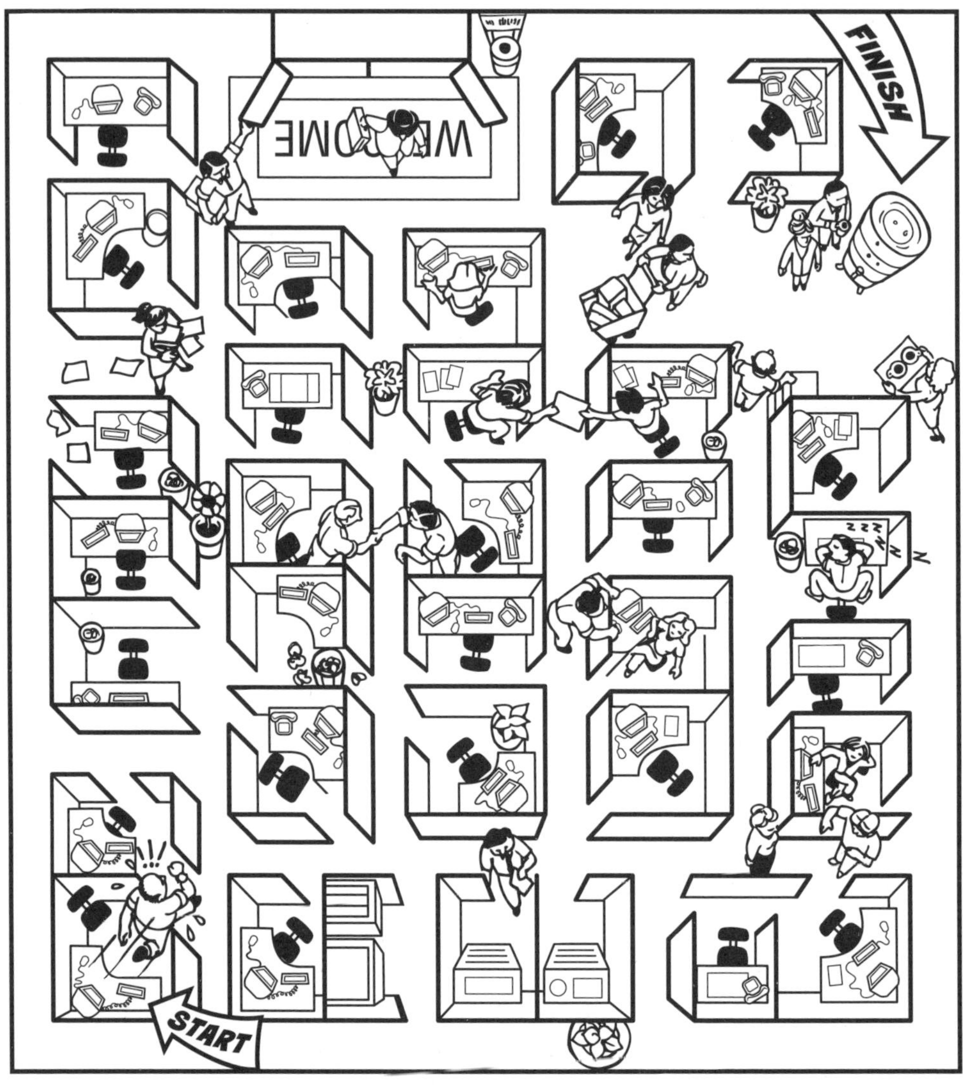

Answer on page 182.

Red, White, and Blue

LOGIC

Each row, column, and long diagonal contains 2 red squares, 2 white squares, and 2 blue squares. From the clues given below, can you complete the grid?

	A	B	C	D	E	F
1						
2						
3						
4						
5						
6						

1. The reds are next to each other.
2. One of the blues is bounded by 2 whites.
3. The blues are somewhere between the whites.
4. One of the reds is bounded by 2 whites.
5. One blue has a red directly to its left, and the other blue has a red directly to its right.
6. The pattern in cells A, B, and C is repeated in D, E, and F.

A. The reds are somewhere between the blues.
B. The blues are next to each other.
C. One blue is bounded by 2 reds and the other by 2 whites.
D. The pattern in cells 1, 2, and 3 is repeated in 4, 5, and 6.
E. The whites are somewhere between the blues.
F. All the blues and reds are between the whites.

Hints: Write the possibilities in small letters until a picture emerges. For example: "The blues are between the whites" means that the 2 outside squares can be only red or white. Don't forget that the 2 long diagonals contain only 2 cells of each color.

Answers on page 182.

My Thoughts, Add-xactly!

COMPUTATION LOGIC

Fill each empty square of the grid with a digit from 1 through 9. When the numbers in each row are added, you should arrive at the total in the right-hand column. When the numbers in each column are added, you should arrive at the total on the bottom line. The numbers in each diagonal must add up to the totals in the upper and lower right corners.

									47
	6		6	9	3	6	5	4	44
7		8		3	2	1	9	2	50
6	2		5		3	5	6	3	33
5	8	9		9		4	8	7	65
1	4	8	5		5		1	9	38
9	5	6	3	2		9		1	46
3	1	7	9	7	9		7		55
	2	8	1	2	2	8		4	39
6		6		7	5	7	1	5	44
44	40	58	49	43	45	46	46	43	45

Volume on the Rise

In the last 3 to 4 million years, brain volume within the hominid lineage has increased from less than 400 milliliters to roughly 1,400 milliliters.

Answers on page 182.

From Adore to Scorn

LANGUAGE PLANNING

Change just one letter on each line to go from the top word to the bottom word. Do not change the order of the letters. You must have a common English a word at each step.

ADORE

______

______

SCORN

Rectangle Roundup

ATTENTION

How many rectangles do you count?

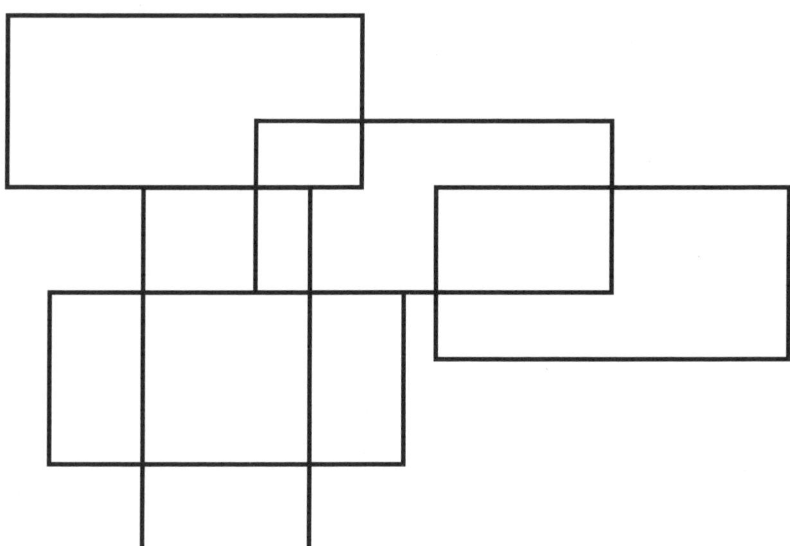

Answers on page 182.

Find It

ATTENTION | GENERAL KNOWLEDGE | LANGUAGE | VISUAL SEARCH

This is a word search with an added twist. Instead of a list of words to find, we've provided a list of categories. Your challenge is to find 3 items for each category within the box of letters below. The words can be found horizontally, vertically, or diagonally. They may read either backward or forward.

3 flowers

3 black things

3 sports

3 hard-to-find things

3 Army ranks

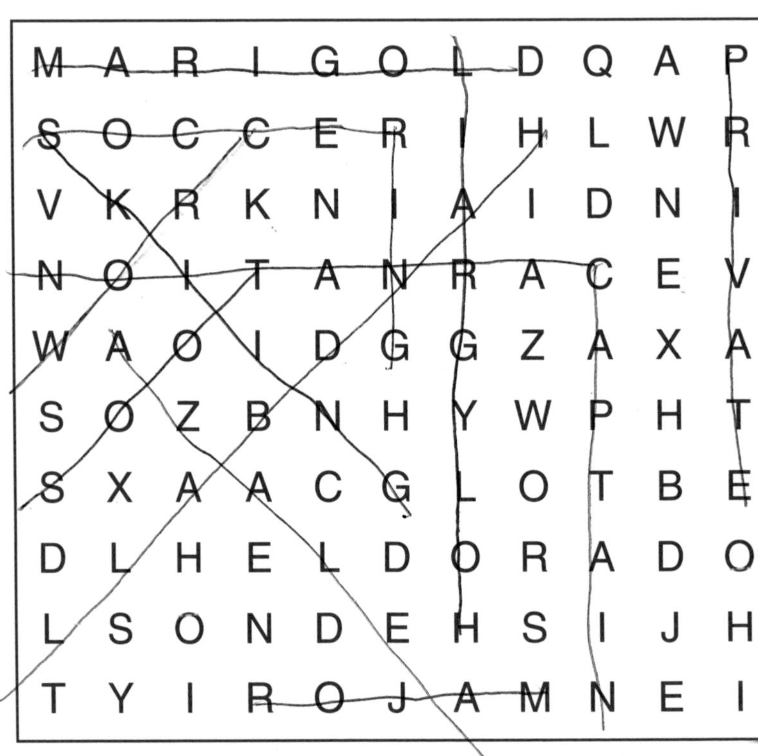

Answers on page 183.

Level 4

Anagram President

LANGUAGE

Find a 5-letter anagram for each of the words below. The anagrams will answer the clues. Write the correct anagram on the line by each clue. When completed correctly, the first letter of the anagrams will spell the name of a United States president.

Anagram Words

REBUT LATER HYDRA SIREN PLANE

UNBAR BLAME LEMON LAYER BURMA SNAKY

Clues

1. Strong: ________
2. Stroll: ________
3. Latin dance: ________
4. Washer cycle: ________
5. Jerks: ________
6. Potato, e.g.: ________
7. ________ race
8. Of the city: ________
9. Large fruit: ________
10. Change: ________
11. Katmandu's country: ________

President: __ __ __ __ __   __ __ __ __ __ __

Answers on page 183.

Star Power

LOGIC

Fill each of the empty squares in the grid so that every starred square is surrounded by a digit from 1 through 8 with no repeats.

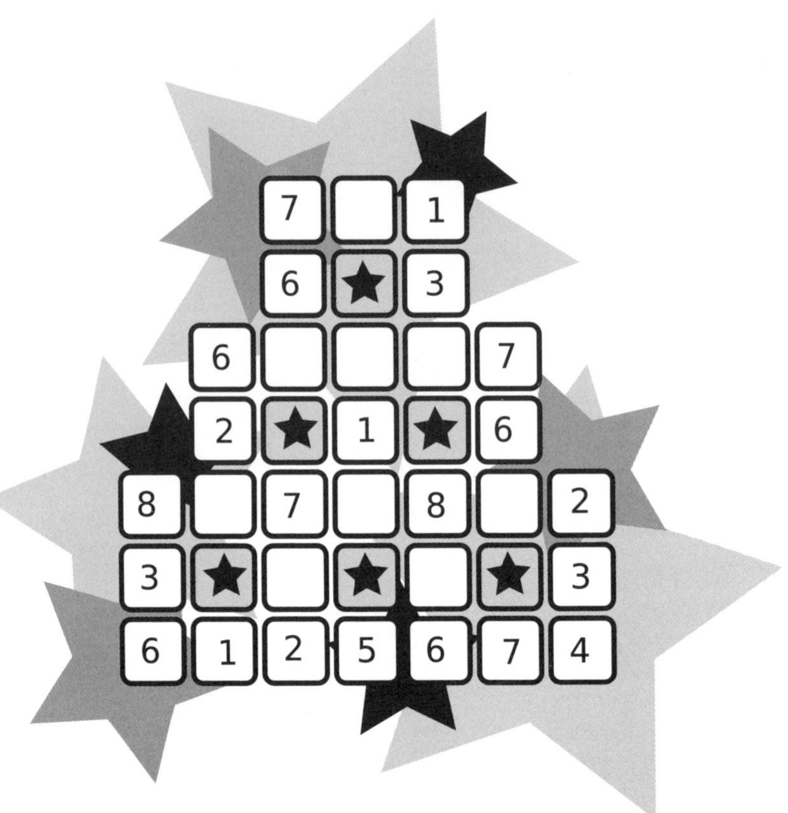

Brain-Friendly Foods

Some research suggests foods containing choline, such as soy, peanuts, and eggs, may help improve alertness and memory and relieve stress. Choline helps build the neurotransmitters that pass electrical impulses between brain cells.

Answers on page 183.

Level 4

Word Paths

LANGUAGE PLANNING

Each of these word paths contains a familiar saying. To figure out the saying, read freely from letter to letter. Some letters will be used more than once. You can also move both forward and backward along the straight lines. The blanks indicate the number of letters in each word of the saying.

1. **2.**

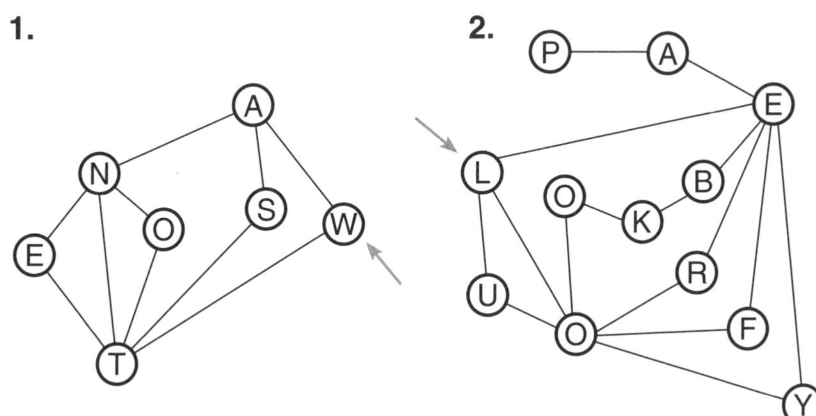

1.

_ _ _ _ _ _   _ _ _

_ _ _ _   _ _ _

2.

_ _ _ _

_ _ _ _ _ _ _   _ _ _

_ _ _ _

3.

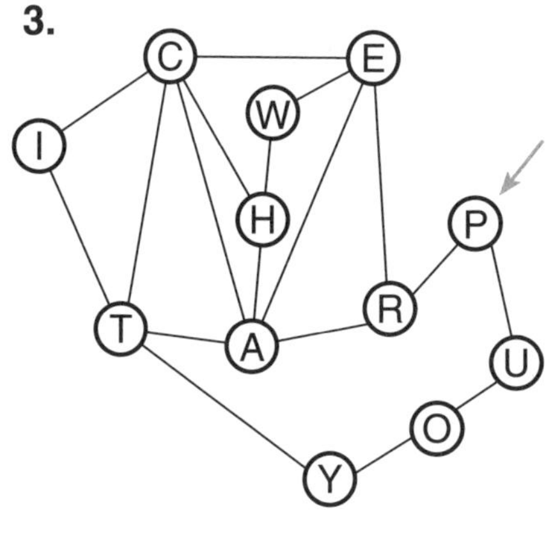

_ _ _ _ _ _ _ _ _

_ _ _ _   _ _ _

_ _ _ _ _ _ _

4.

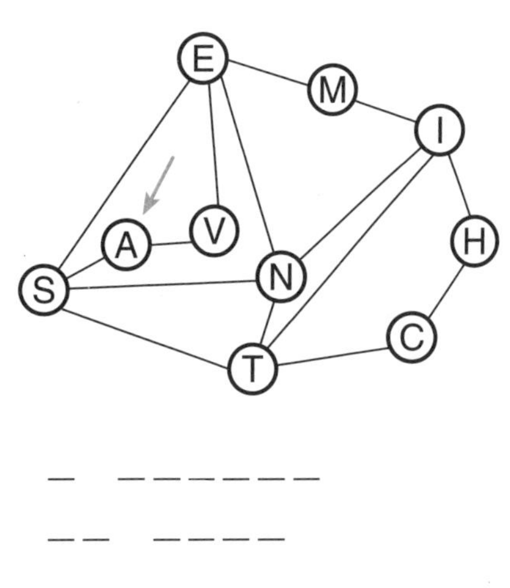

_   _ _ _ _ _ _ _

_ _   _ _ _ _ _

_ _ _ _ _   _ _ _ _

Answers on page 183.

Menagerie Nursery

GENERAL KNOWLEDGE | LANGUAGE

Across

1. Skating event
6. Rick's "Casablanca" love
10. Door feature
14. Comedian Murphy
15. Former Georgia senator
16. College in New Rochelle
17. It's below the knee
19. Lara Croft raids it
20. Short joke
21. Knockout drink
23. Hot under the collar
24. City on the Po River
26. Was in session
27. Thankless one
31. The Pips, to Gladys Knight
35. Hits the roof
36. Utah's Hatch
37. Little boy
38. Youth with a lamp
41. Suitability
43. Iceberg alternative
44. Swedish flier
45. Palindromic vehicle
47. Melville captain
51. Seaport of Italia
54. Phone call opener
56. Citizens' rights group: abbr.
57. Revolver maker
59. It smooths things over
60. German auto
61. March honoree, familiarly: abbr.
62. Off-color
63. Part in a play
64. Actor Davis

Down

1. River to the Rio Grande
2. Hersey's "A Bell for _____"
3. Time waster
4. Biathlon weapon
5. Prefix with "sweet"
6. Newspaper pullouts
7. Monetary gain
8. Weekend TV comedy show
9. Flower or swimmer
10. Scout of the Old West
11. Secluded spot
12. Round-buyer's words
13. Diaper wearer
18. Take the lid off
22. Swallows
25. Prefix with place or print
26. Old timer
28. Composer Thomas

29. Cash-register section
30. Ice-cream brand
31. Sow's mate
32. Alice's Restaurant patron
33. To overcrowd
34. Engage in horseplay
39. Tooth for gnawing
40. Name divider
41. In general
42. French capital, in song
46. Water-conserving critter
47. Bank units: abbr.
48. Gym game
49. Ike's opponent
50. Actress Davis
51. Execute perfectly, slang
52. Approx. 4,047 square meters
53. Clear snow-covered roads
55. Furthermore
58. GI mail drop

Answers on page 183.

Alphabet Puzzle

PLANNING | SPATIAL REASONING

To solve this puzzle, move in alphabetical order in a single, unbroken path from A to Z. You can't move diagonally—only vertically or horizontally. There's only one way to do it.

A	B	C	D	E	O	I	M	N	O	P
B	G	D	E	L	M	N	O	P	U	Q
C	F	E	J	K	L	G	R	Q	T	R
D	G	H	I	N	M	Q	Q	R	S	U
E	L	I	J	O	N	O	P	Q	R	S
F	G	J	K	P	O	S	T	U	W	T
G	H	S	L	R	P	Q	R	S	V	F
J	I	N	M	N	Q	R	U	T	U	V
W	V	O	T	O	R	S	T	U	R	W
X	W	V	U	P	U	T	X	V	U	X
Y	X	W	V	W	V	W	V	U	V	Y
S	Y	X	W	S	T	V	W	X	Y	Z

Logidoku

LOGIC

The numbers 1 to 9 appear once in every row, column, long diagonal, irregular shape, and 3×3 grid. From the numbers given, can you complete the puzzle?

Answers on page 183.

Star Power

LOGIC

Fill in each of the empty squares in the grid so that every starred square is surrounded by a digit from 1 through 8 with no repeats.

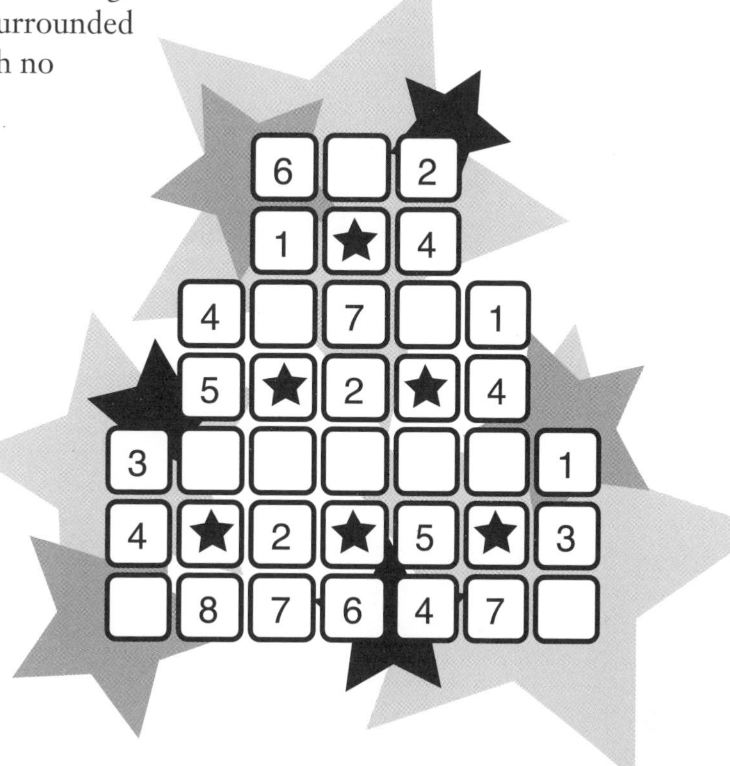

Geometric Shapes

PLANNING

SPATIAL VISUALIZATION

Divide the whole grid into smaller geometric shapes by drawing straight lines that follow either the full grid lines or the full diagonals of the square cells. Each formed shape must have exactly one symbol inside, which represents it but might not look identical to it.

Hints: The rectangle symbol cannot be contained in a square. Each trapezoid has 2 sides parallel, but its other 2 sides are not parallel.

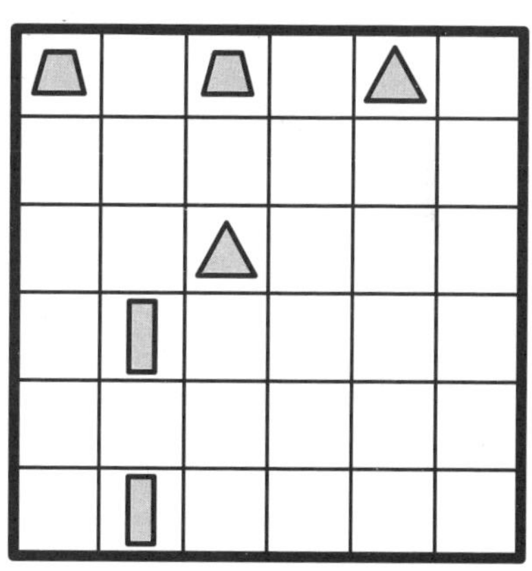

Answers on page 183.

Sudoku

LOGIC

To solve a sudoku puzzle, place the numbers 1 through 9 only once in each row, column, and 3×3 box. Each puzzle has some numbers filled in—you just need to work out the rest. You'll never have to guess; all the puzzles can be solved using the power of deduction.

				2			6	
7		8	1					3
	4		5			1		
1	3			4				
				5				
				7			2	1
		7			5		8	
5					4	9		6
	6			8				

Number Crossword

COMPUTATION LOGIC

Use the clues to determine which of the digits 1 through 9 belongs in each square in the diagram. Digits may be repeated within a number, and no zeros are used.

Across

1. The sum of its digits is 10
3. Even digits, in some order
6. Consecutive odd digits, descending
7. A multiple of 17

Down

1. A perfect square
2. Consecutive digits, ascending
4. A palindrome
5. An odd number

1	2	■	■
3		4	5
6			
■	■	7	

Answers on page 184.

Variety of V's

ATTENTION | VISUAL SEARCH

You'll find a variety of things in this picture that begin with the letter **V.** We count 10. How many do you see?

What Month's Next?

ANALYSIS | CREATIVE THINKING

What month comes next in this sequence?

APRIL, AUGUST, DECEMBER, FEBRUARY, _____

Answers on page 184.

Mirror, Mirror

SPATIAL VISUALIZATION

There's no trick here, only a challenge: Draw the mirror image of each of these familiar objects. You may find it harder than you think!

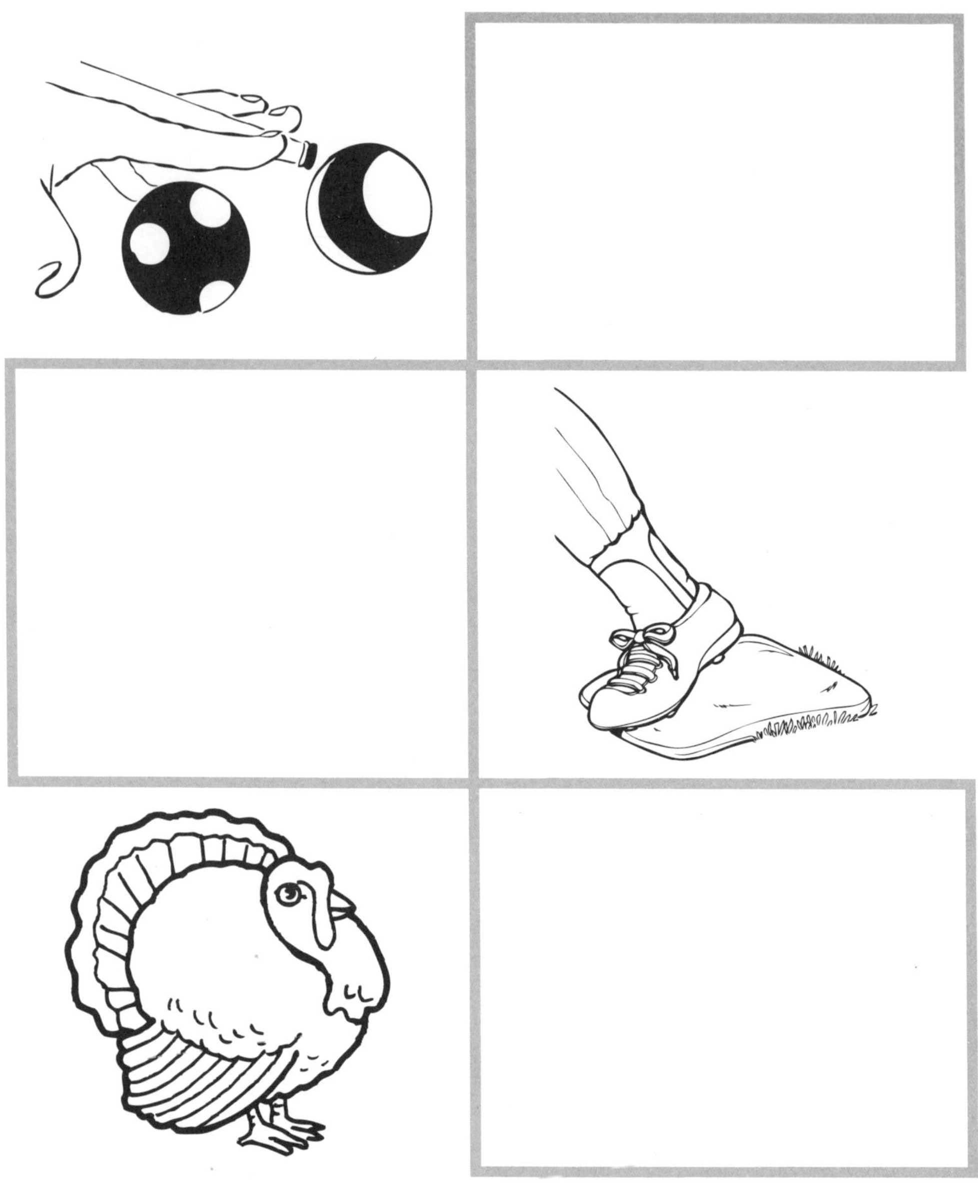

Logidoku

LOGIC

The numbers 1 to 9 appear once in every row, column, long diagonal, irregular shape, and 3×3 grid. From the numbers given, can you complete the puzzle?

				5		4		
	7				8			
								7
						1		
	6							
				3			5	
9								
				8			9	
	1							2

Fitting Words

LANGUAGE LOGIC PLANNING

In this miniature crossword, the clues are listed randomly and are numbered for convenience only. It is up to you to figure out the placement of the 9 answers. To help you out, we've inserted one letter in the grid, and this is the *only* occurrence of that letter in the completed puzzle.

Clues

1. Academy Award, for example
2. Academy Award winner, perhaps
3. Visionary
4. Band gear
5. Label information
6. Accumulate
7. Hungry
8. Meal with matzoh
9. Seconds

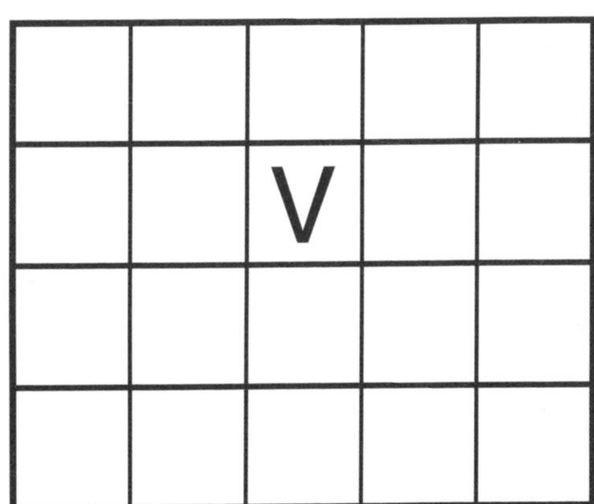

Answers on page 184.

Rhyme Time

GENERAL KNOWLEDGE | LANGUAGE

Answer each clue below with a pair of rhyming words. The numbers that follow each clue indicate how many letters are in each word. For example, "Cookware taken straight from the oven (3, 3)" would be "hot pot."

1. Special occasion at the aquarium (3, 3): ______________________
2. Record of online journal entries (4, 3): ______________________
3. A midnight snack, for example (5, 4): ______________________
4. Backward kicker's aid (5, 4): ______________________
5. Part of a pol's preparation (5, 5): ______________________
6. Mark of the biggest Texas ranch (5, 5): ______________________
7. Brit's unexpected discovery (5, 5): ______________________
8. Auto museum (6, 4): ______________________
9. Bobsledder's favorite spot (6, 4): ______________________
10. Retaliate (6, 4): ______________________
11. Prepare to tie (5, 6): ______________________
12. Mass participant (6, 5): ______________________
13. Thanksgiving meat, cut and dried (6, 5): ______________________
14. She hoards cleaning devices (7, 6): ______________________
15. Suggest the plan (7, 9): ______________________

Answers on page 184.

A Lark in the Park

There are 14 differences between the top and bottom park scenes. Can you spot all of them?

Answers on page 184.

Curvaceous Cube Construction

SPATIAL REASONING

Which one of the cubes can be made from the unfolded sample?

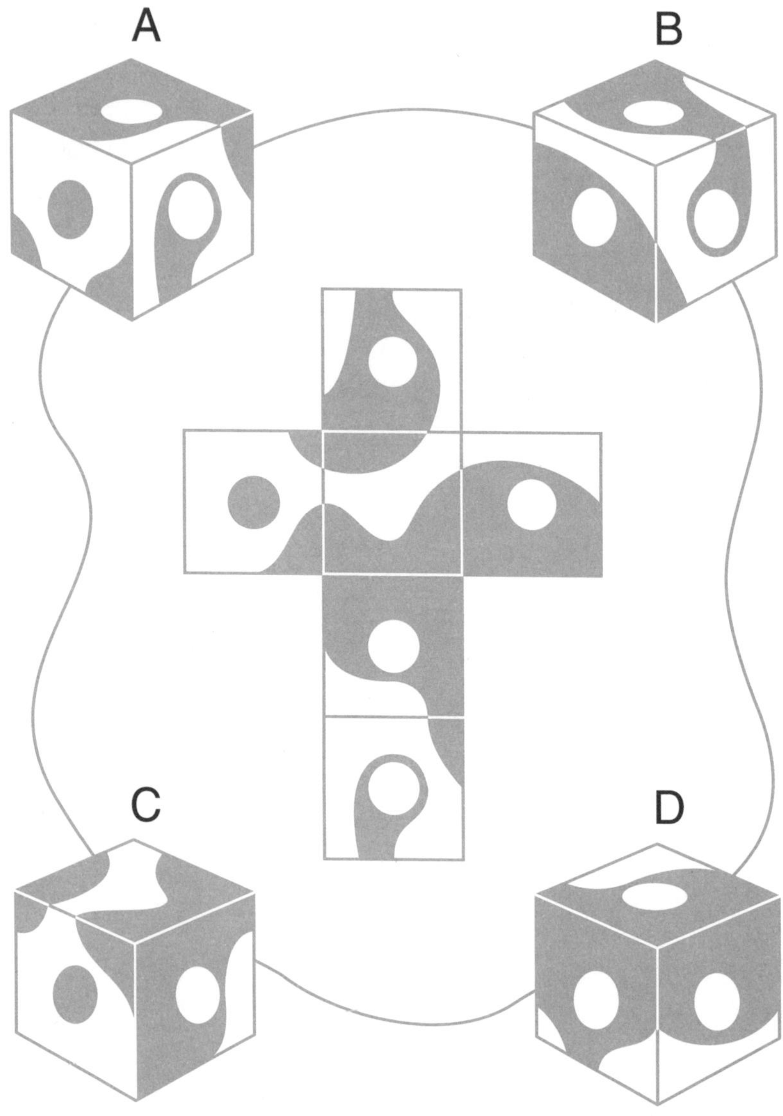

Answer on page 184.

A Word to the Wise

LANGUAGE

In the line below, cross out 12 letters in such a way that the remaining letters spell a common word.

SEAVCOEMNMLOENTWOTERRDS

Odd-Even Logidoku

LOGIC

The numbers 1 to 9 are to appear once in every row, column, long diagonal, irregular shape, and 3×3 grid. Cells marked with the letter **E** contain even numbers. From the numbers given, can you complete the puzzle?

			E		E	E		E
E		E		E		9		E
E	E		1	E			E	
E			E				8	E
	5	E	E	E		E		
E		E			E	E		
3	E	E	E			7		2
	E				E	E	E	
	E			E	4		E	

Answers on page 184.

Ovoids Maze

PLANNING SPATIAL REASONING

Answer on page 185.

Fitting Words

LANGUAGE LOGIC PLANNING

In this miniature crossword, the clues are listed randomly and are numbered for convenience only. It is up to you to figure out the placement of the 9 answers. To help you out, we've inserted one letter in the grid, and this is the *only* occurrence of that letter in the completed puzzle.

Clues

1. Boring item
2. Nimble
3. Floor coverings
4. Greenish-blue
5. Foul
6. Try to lose
7. Outfit
8. Poets
9. Hit on the noggin

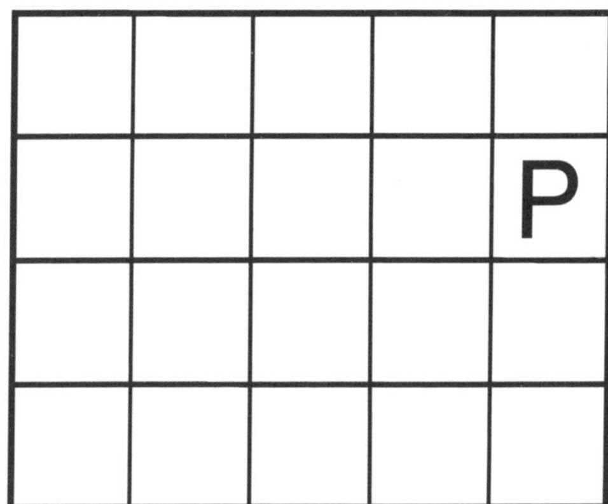

Geometric Shapes

SPATIAL REASONING

Divide the grid into smaller geometric shapes by drawing straight lines that follow either the full grid lines or the full diagonals of the square cells. Each formed shape must have exactly one symbol inside, which represents it but might not look identical to it. When the puzzle is solved, all of the grid will be used.

Hint: Each trapezoid has 2 sides parallel, but its other 2 sides are not parallel.

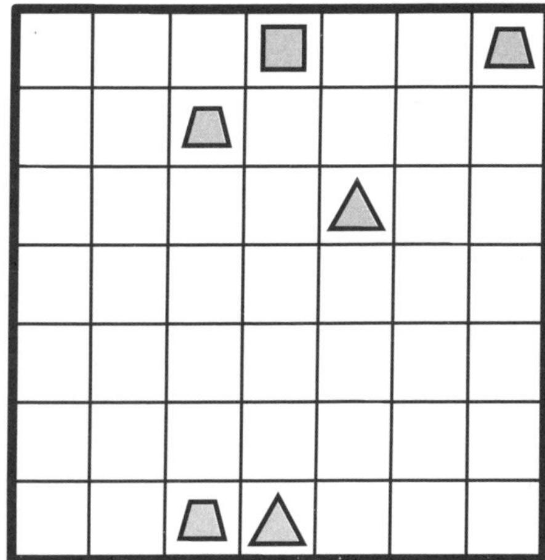

Answers on page 185.

H. H.

ATTENTION LANGUAGE VISUAL SEARCH

Every word listed is contained within the group of letters on page 129. The words can be found horizontally, vertically, or diagonally. They may read either backward or forward.

HADDON HALL
HA-HA'S
HALFHEARTED
HALF HITCH
HALF HOUR
HAM-HANDED
HAMMERHEAD
HANDHOLDS
HAPHAZARD
HARDHACK
HARDHEAD
HARD-HITTING
HARTSHORN
HARVEST HOME
HAZEL HEN
HEADHUNTER
HEATH HEN
HEAVY-HANDED
HEDDA HOPPER
HEDGEHOG
HEE-HAW
HEIGH-HO
HELEN HAYES
HEXAHEDRON
HIGH HOLIDAY
HITCHHIKE
HOBBYHORSE
HOGSHEAD
HO HO
HO-HUM
HOLLYHOCK
HOMO HABILIS
HOPHEAD
HOP HORNBEAM
HOREHOUND
HORSEHAIR
HORSEHIDE
HOTHOUSE
HOUSEHOLD
HULL HOUSE
HUNTING HORNS

The leftover letters will tell you where hurricanes hardly ever happen (3 words).

```
Y H G R H S R                       H E H K H N H
A O N E A D U                       E S O C I O A
D M I T P L O                       D U U O T R L
I O T N H O H                       G O S H C D F
L H T U A H F                       E H E Y H E H
O A I H Z D L                       H T H L H H E
H B H D A N A                       O O O L I A A
H I D A R A H E H H C T I H F L A H G H L O K X R
G L R E D H E R H T H U L L H O U S E F D H E E T
I I A H A M H A N D E D S N R O H G N I T N U H E
H S H A R I A H E S R O H A Z E L H E N O M H E D
A E O R R D H A R D H A C K A H P E N N R U O A A
D Y B V D N U O H E R O H D E F O P R E R H P V E
D A B E D I H E S R O H M A E B N R O H P O H Y H
O H Y S D S E                       H H W H E H R
N N H T A A I                       S T A N A A E
H E O H D H G                       T A H D D N M
A L R O O A H                       R E E H D D M
L E S M A H H                       A H E M P E A
L H E E S H O                       H I H R E D H
```

Leftover letters spell: ____________________

About Sleep

By the time you are 80 years old, you will have spent more than 233,600 hours sleeping! That's the equivalent of 26.67 years.

Answers on page 185.

Greedy Gears

COMPUTATION

Place a number between the spokes of each gear so that digits across from each other add up to the number on the gear and also follow the rules on the gear spokes concerning greater-than or less-than symbols. In the spaces where the spokes of gear 6 are within the gaps of the other gears, assume the digit is 6. Digits may be used more than once on the same gear if necessary but may not be placed next to each other.

Sudoku

LOGIC

To solve a sudoku puzzle, place the numbers 1 through 9 only once in each row, column, and 3×3 box. Each puzzle has some numbers filled in—you just need to work out the rest. You'll never have to guess; all the puzzles can be solved using the power of deduction.

			4	7				
			3			5	8	
	6					3		7
7			1			8		
5				3				6
		4			7			2
2		8					4	
	1	3			8			
				2	1			

Answers on page 185.

Sketchbook

MEMORY

Ambrose Anderson's granddaughter loved to draw. When she came home, she'd draw everything she could remember seeing that day. The top picture is a page from her sketchbook. Later on, she erased 3 of the drawings and replaced them with 3 new drawings. Study the top picture carefully, then turn the page upside down to check out her revised sketchbook page. Without looking back at the top picture, can you circle the 3 drawings that are different?

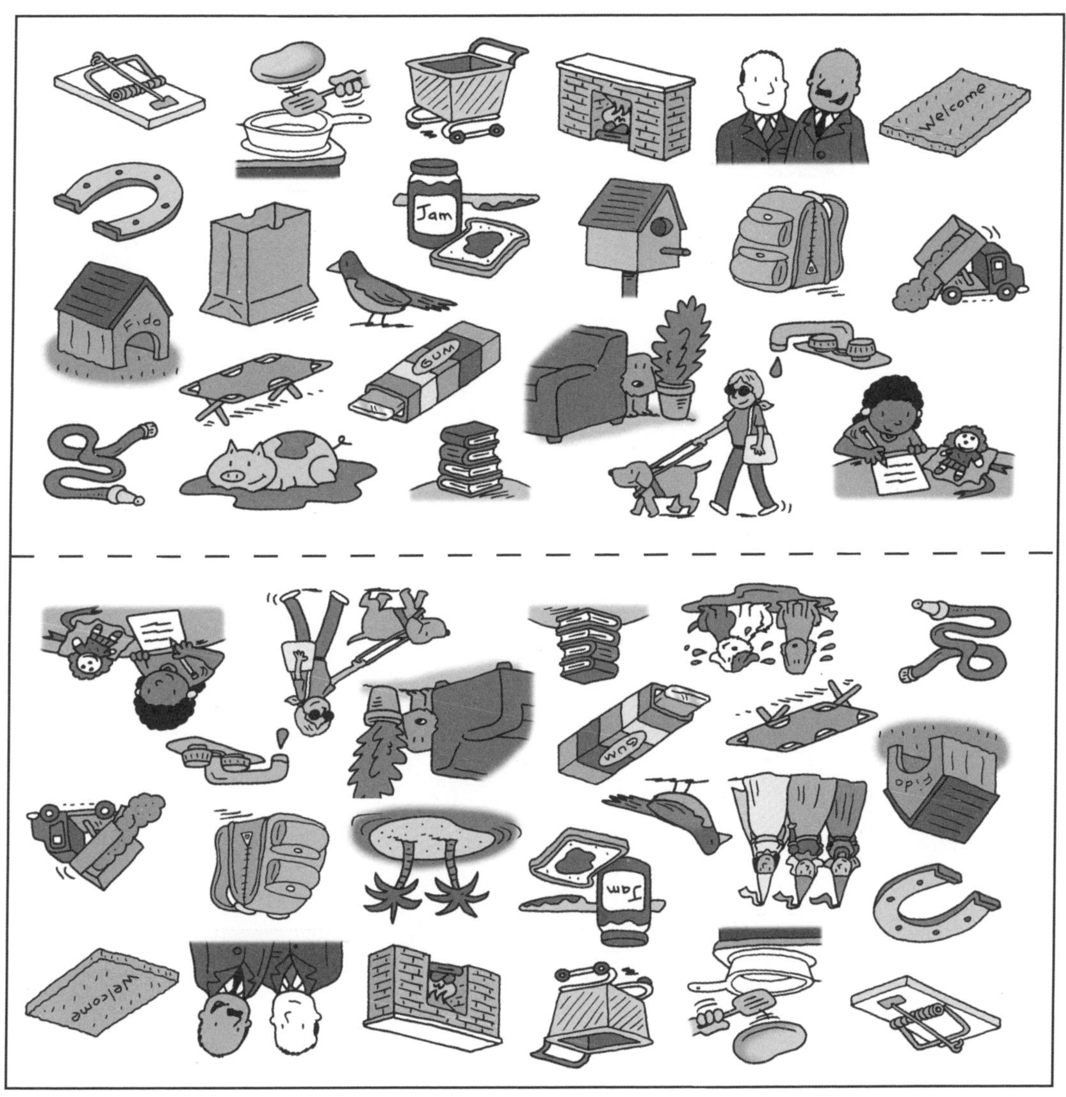

Answers on page 186.

Hexagonal Shift

PLANNING SPATIAL REASONING

Get It?

LANGUAGE

Can you "read" the phrase below?

IIIIIIIIIIIIIITTTTTTTTTT

it

Answers on page 186.

Bungled Burglary

ATTENTION

We count 17 things wrong with this picture. Can you find them?

Answers on page 186.

Temperature's Rising

GENERAL KNOWLEDGE | LANGUAGE

Across

1. Bush and Clinton
5. "No, thanks"
10. Spike, as a drink
14. Late-night host Jay
15. _____ Vader of "Star Wars"
16. Israel's Abba
17. One way to quit
19. Pita sandwich
20. With all sincerity
21. Drizzles
22. Old Nissan
23. Wrangler's rope
24. Tidy Lotto prize
29. Licorice-flavored plant
33. Roulette bet
34. Ballerina Pavlova
35. Dryer-trap content
36. Molten material
37. Echelon
38. Court minutes
39. "Would _____?"
40. Willing and able partner
41. Reception with open arms
44. Turn edible
45. Song title that means "you are" in Spanish
50. Diamond side
51. Prelate's title
54. "Yikes!"
55. Showing off
56. Publisher Henry
57. Of interest to Audubon
58. Slight advantage
59. Sets down
60. Office furniture
61. Type of ringer

Down

1. Spanish hero
2. Former hotelier Helmsley
3. Narrow waterway
4. Bubbly drinks
5. Phrase said with a shrug
6. Skin
7. Torah storers
8. Editor's "put it back in"
9. Like a shrinking violet
10. Pass laws
11. Ethiopia, formerly
12. Drew "Doonesbury," e.g.
13. Baseball Hall of Famer Slaughter
18. Cease-fire
21. Prefix with function
23. Former coin of Italy
25. Words before fours
26. Line of thinking

27. Old-style copier
28. Quaint negative
29. "There oughta be _____."
30. Costa Rica neighbor
31. Complex nature
32. Herd panics
36. Bearing
40. Equip anew
42. Freshly painted
43. Subatomic particles
46. Goaded, with "on"
47. Rudely sarcastic
48. Polynesian kingdom
49. Dangled a carrot before
50. Cut down
51. Chess action
52. Elevator man
53. Fargo's state: abbr.
55. Fooled

Answers on page 186.

The Times Are Changing!

COMPUTATION **LOGIC**

Fill in the missing spaces with numbers from 1 to 5. When multiplied together, the numbers in each row should produce the totals on the right, the numbers in each column should produce the totals at the bottom, and the corner-to-corner diagonals should produce the totals in the upper and lower right corners.

					20
	4	5	3	2	240
	3	3	5	5	225
	3	1		4	96
	2	5	4	1	120
	3	4	2	2	48
12	216	300	480	80	48

Perfect Sunday Picnic?

ATTENTION

Ellen and Jim wanted everything to be perfect this afternoon, but it looks like it didn't quite work out. We count 8 wrong things in this picture. How many can you find?

Answers on page 186.

FEEL THE BURN

LEVEL 5

Arrows

PLANNING

SPATIAL REASONING

Draw one arrow in each of the empty squares surrounding the number grid. Each arrow should be positioned horizontally, vertically, or diagonally so that it points to at least 1 cell inside the grid. The number in each cell shows how many arrows should be pointing to it when all of the squares have been filled in.

1	4	3	5
1	3	3	6
1	3	4	4
2	6	3	4

Sudoku

LOGIC

To solve a sudoku puzzle, place the numbers 1 through 9 only once in each row, column, and 3×3 box. Each puzzle has some numbers filled in—you just need to work out the rest. You'll never have to guess; all the puzzles can be solved using the power of deduction.

	7			9	3	4	2	
		8						3
					1			
		5	1					4
		9		2		6		
6					4	5		
			6					
7						1		
	4	6	5	1			9	

Answers on pages 186–187.

A Beast of a Word Ladder!

LANGUAGE PLANNING

Change just one letter on each line to go from the top word to the bottom word. Do not change the order of the letters. You must have a word at each step.

BEAST

____

____

____

____

____

____

____

____

____

SAINT

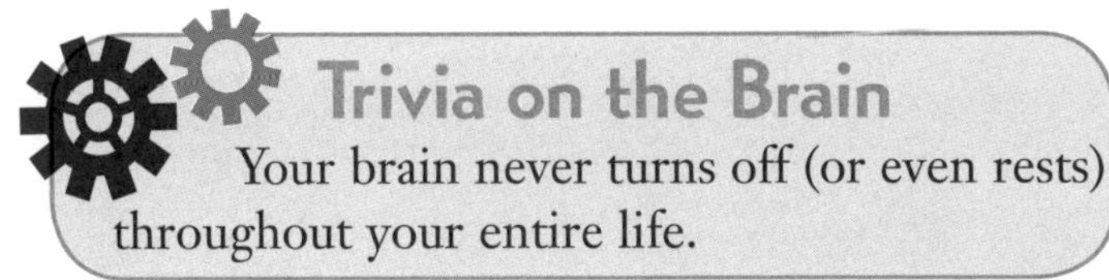

Trivia on the Brain

Your brain never turns off (or even rests) throughout your entire life.

Answers on page 187.

Level 5

Rhyme Time

GENERAL KNOWLEDGE | LANGUAGE

Answer each clue below with a pair of rhyming words. The numbers that follow each clue indicate how many letters are in each word. For example, "Cookware taken straight from the oven (3, 3)" would be "hot pot."

1. Clever bargain (3, 3): ______________
2. Food for baby bears (3, 4): ______________
3. Mouthwash pioneer (6, 6): ______________
4. Club's posting about charges (4, 4): ______________
5. Where the plane crossed Delaware (4, 5): ______________
6. Cook a meat no one will eat (4, 5): ______________
7. A breakfast record (4, 5): ______________
8. An invitation to play rugby (4, 5): ______________
9. A more intelligent group of fish (5, 4): ______________
10. Bicycle-shop offering (5, 4): ______________
11. Easy pace at the outset of the race (5, 5): ______________
12. It's part of a coven's recruiting (5, 5): ______________
13. Make a raid in the dairy section (5, 6): ______________
14. Get along really well (6, 5): ______________
15. Silly wall painting (7, 5): ______________
16. Top-ranking emcee (8, 4): ______________
17. Incense holder used for decades (7, 8): ______________
18. A study of new paragraphs (11, 11): ______________
19. Investigator who looks inward (13, 9): ______________
20. Ad of questionable taste (13, 10): ______________

Answers on page 187.

How to Turn a Lemon into an Apple

LANGUAGE PLANNING

This is a word ladder with an anagramming twist. To get to each step of the ladder, change one letter in the previous word. Then rearrange the letters to form a new word.

Are you up to the challenge?

LEMON

____

____

APPLE

Word Jigsaw

SPATIAL PLANNING

Fit the pieces into the frame to form common, uncapitalized words reading across and down crossword-style. There's no need to rotate the pieces; they'll fit as shown, with each piece used exactly once.

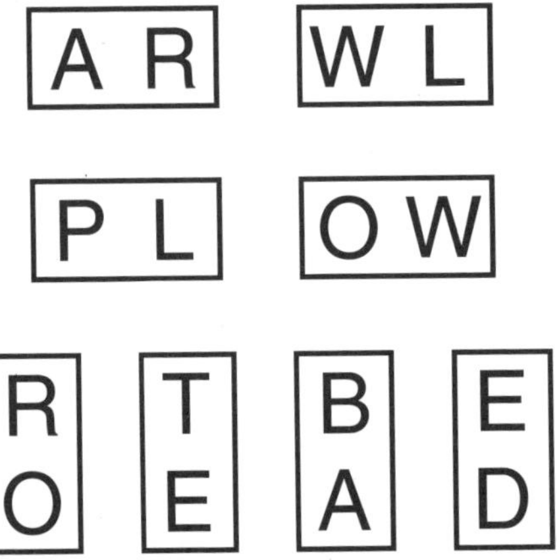

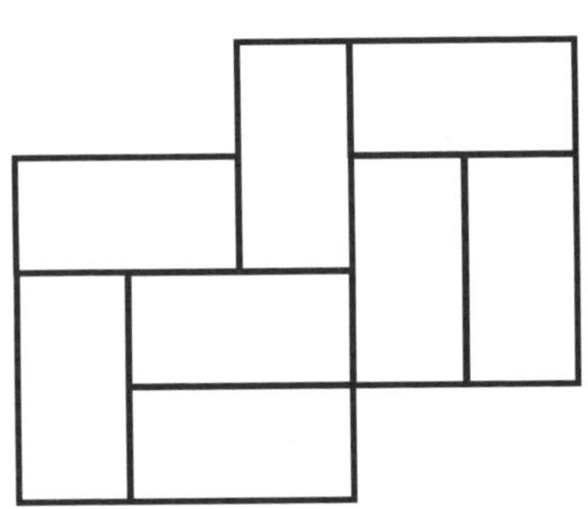

Answers on page 187.

Milky Way

LOGIC

Exactly 2 stars are hidden in each row and in each column of the map. The stars do not touch each other, not even diagonally. Find the stars.

Geometric Shapes

LOGIC

SPATIAL REASONING

Divide the whole grid into smaller geometric shapes by drawing straight lines that follow either the full grid lines or the full diagonals of the square cells. Each formed shape must have exactly one symbol inside, which represents it but might not look identical to it. When the puzzle is solved, all of the grid will be used.

Hints: The parallelogram is not inside a square. The trapezoid has two sides parallel, but its other two sides are not parallel.

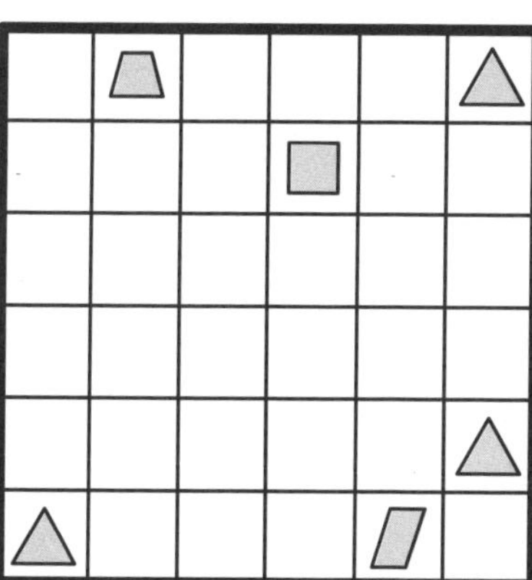

Answers on page 187.

Four Magic Words

GENERAL KNOWLEDGE

LANGUAGE

This puzzle is a wacky take on a crossword puzzle. Follow the clues to fill in the puzzle grid. We've done one for you. All the clues for this puzzle are within the grid. If you answer them correctly, 4 unclued words will appear in the shaded areas.

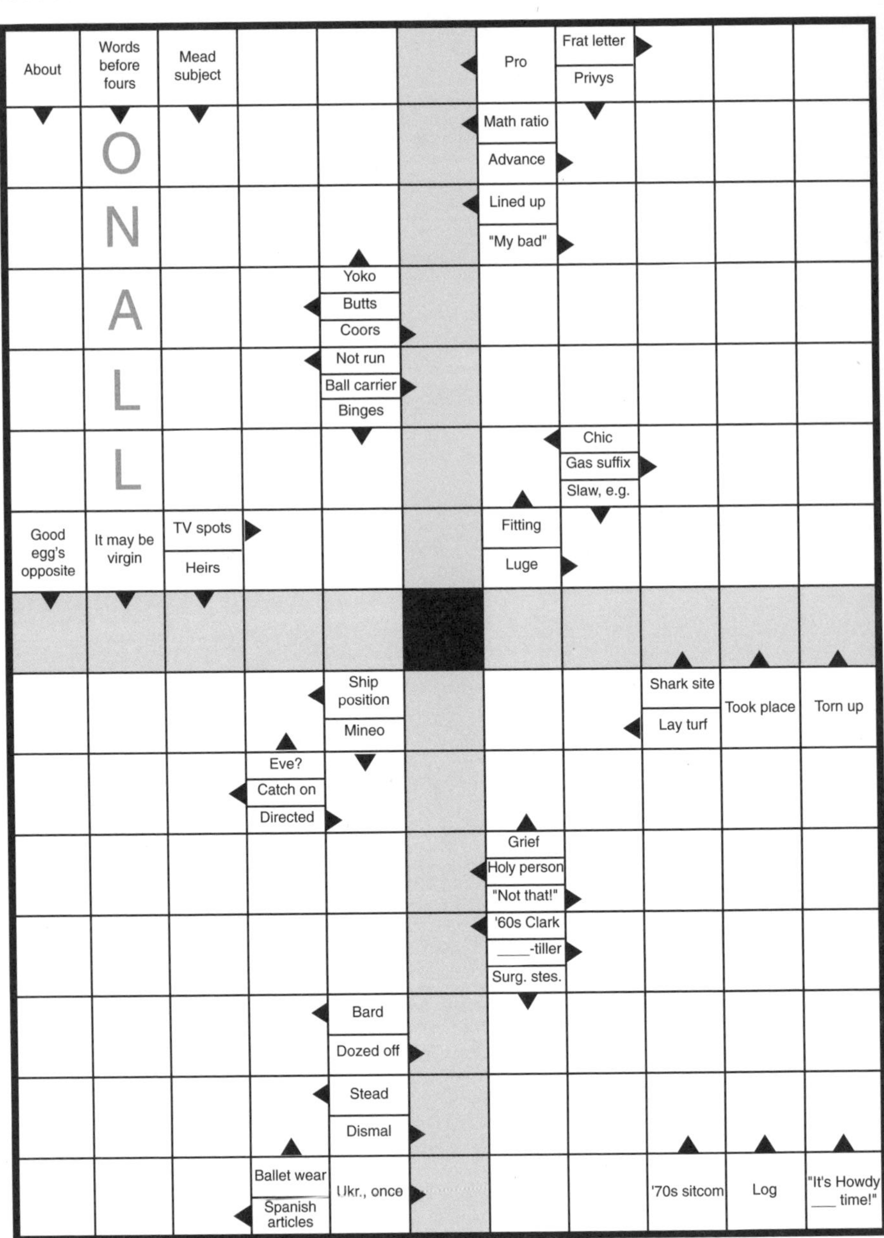

Answers on page 187.

Look at that Charter Cutie!

LANGUAGE

Can you rearrange the letters of the capitalized words to make a new word that actually makes sense? Here's a clue: These are anagrams about ARCHITECTURE.

Teaching a course in TRITE CHAUCER ________________, the professor said, "Consider the CARGO HITCH ________________, often seen in churches and stained-glass windows. Or you might see it in a COSTLIER ________________, a protected type of place. Now, when it comes to classical columns, my personal favorite is the CHARIOT INN ________________. A column, statue, or vase often rests on a STEEL PAD ________________. A slightly projecting column built onto or against a wall? Believe it or not, that's a LASER TIP __________. For next class, study up on the flying BUST REST ________________, which isn't quite what you young men are thinking!"

As the students filed out, a stony ROYAL EGG ________________, jutting from the parapet of a building across the quad, grinned fiercely down at them.

How Your Body Reacts to Pain

If you are involved in a serious accident, your survival system is so busy that you hardly feel any pain even though you may be severely injured. If, however, you know you've been exposed to someone with a condition such as chicken pox, the slightest sensation on your skin may feel like an itchy pain because you are expecting to feel it.

Answers on page 187.

Presidential Portraits

GENERAL KNOWLEDGE | LANGUAGE

Across

1. Yawn-inducing
5. Wren or hen
9. Mushroom-cloud maker
14. College in New Rochelle
15. Buffalo's lake
16. Palmer, to pals
17. Collette of "In Her Shoes"
18. Zip
19. Championship
20. First jug at the bar?
23. Failures, in slang
24. Small pooch, briefly
25. Polyester brand
28. Nicholas or Peter
30. Stylish, once
33. Online sales
34. Opportunities for repentance
35. Granada greeting
36. Suffix with Congo
37. Great grade
38. Group of soldiers
39. "The Wizard of Oz" actor
40. One of the Brady Bunch
41. Tylenol alternative
42. Football's Parseghian
43. Methods
44. Took part in the game
45. "Say no more!"
47. Goes out with
48. Storage of angling gear?
55. Ward off
56. Per unit
57. Couple, in a column
58. Joiner's phrase
59. Julia of "The Addams Family"
60. Forum home
61. City on the Ruhr
62. Prime the poker pot
63. High-tech suffix

Down

1. They may be boring
2. Rifle
3. Visitor to Siam
4. Source of hot air
5. Harmless
6. Fairway choices
7. One year in a trunk
8. Heartfelt
9. Carroll's mad tea drinker
10. Building unit
11. Where to see presidential portraits?
12. Denver's elevation, roughly
13. Brewski
21. Screwdriver, e.g.
22. "No, thanks"
25. Perry's secretary
26. On ___ (rampaging)
27. The ability to sing and play guitar, to Johnny?
28. Scrabble pieces

29. Cozy
31. Kind of drab
32. Passé
34. Full of pep
35. Island attire
37. Yawning
41. Obi-Wan player
43. Chinese dumpling
44. Tune from "Funny Girl"
46. Pang
47. Pub potable
48. Celebrity
49. Currier's partner
50. Fictional Georgia plantation
51. Bridge
52. Part of Ripley's phrase
53. Nautilus commander
54. Feds

Answers on page 188.

Quorum of Q's

ATTENTION **VISUAL SEARCH**

There is a quorum of things beginning with the letter **Q** in this picture. We count 6. How many can you find?

Answers on page 188.

Supply Yourself!

ATTENTION

Someone spilled dots of ink all over our office supplies. How many ink dots do you count?

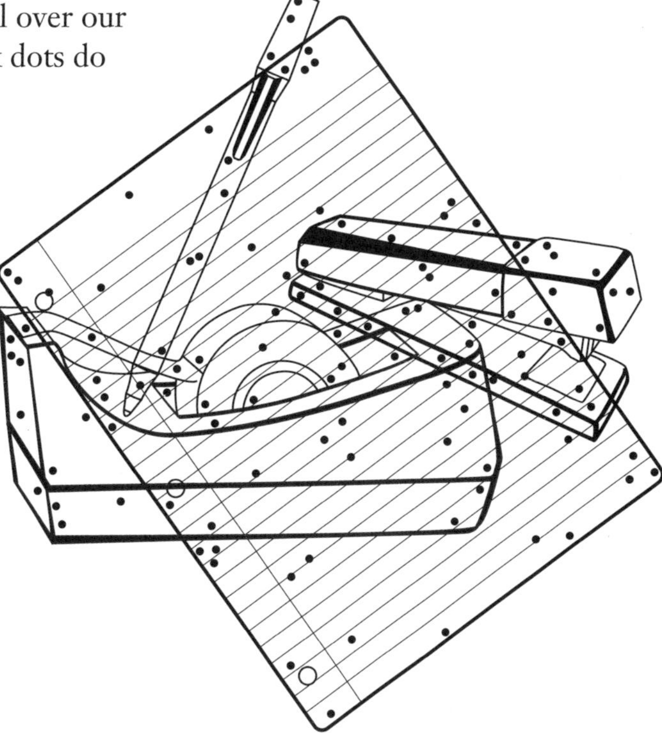

No Business Like Snow Business

COMPUTATION LOGIC

It's snowing like frozen cats and dogs in Cleveland, and the offices of Humanpower Temporary Services have closed for the day so its workers can shovel the snow off their cars and make the slow trek home. Watching from their window in the executive suite, owners Tim and Anna have wagered $100 on whether men or women are the better snow shovelers. They know from last winter, when they were buried in "The Snowstorm that Ate Cleveland," that 10 men and 8 women can shovel as much snow in 12 hours as 8 men and 12 women can shovel in 10 hours. Tim has bet on the men, and Anna has bet on the women. Who are the better workers, and by how much?

Answers on page 188.

Draw This!

SPATIAL VISUALIZATION

There's no trick here, only a challenge: Draw the mirror image of each of these familiar objects. You may find it harder than you think!

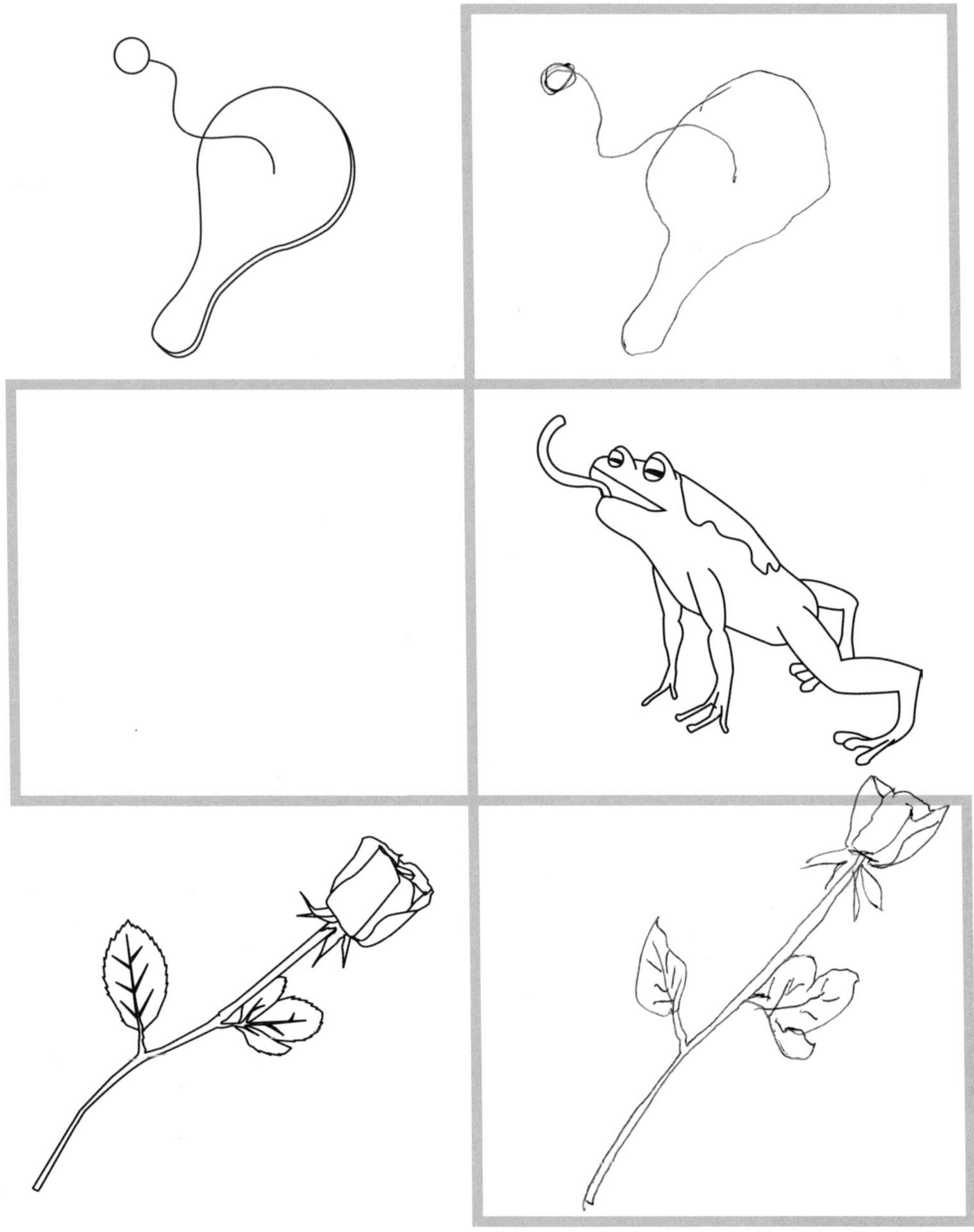

Three Stories

ATTENTION VISUAL SEARCH

Three names are hidden in this grid a total of 94 times. One name is 2 letters long, another is 3 letters long, and the last is 6 letters long. Can you figure out how many times each name appears, reading left to right, right to left, top to bottom, bottom to top, and all 4 ways diagonally?

When you're done, can you find a 4-letter word that's something each of these people might hold? Can you find all 24 places where that word appears in the grid? (Hint: Count both backward and forward.)

Answers on page 188.

Eat Your Words

ATTENTION | LANGUAGE | VISUAL SEARCH

Every phrase listed is contained within the group of letters on the next page. The phrases can be found horizontally, vertically, or diagonally. They may read either backward or forward.

AN APPLE A DAY KEEPS THE DOCTOR AWAY

BRING HOME THE BACON

CAULIFLOWER EAR

COMPARE APPLES AND ORANGES

COOL AS A CUCUMBER

COUCH POTATO

CRY OVER SPILT MILK

A FINE KETTLE OF FISH

FLAT AS A PANCAKE

HAPPY AS A CLAM

I HEARD IT THROUGH THE GRAPEVINE

IN A PICKLE

KNOW YOUR ONIONS

LIKE TWO PEAS IN A POD

NOT MY CUP OF TEA

PIE IN THE SKY

RED AS A BEET

SALT OF THE EARTH

SPILL THE BEANS

THAT'S THE WAY THE COOKIE CRUMBLES

THE PROOF IS IN THE PUDDING

THE WORLD IS YOUR OYSTER

TOP BANANA

WAKE UP AND SMELL THE COFFEE

WORK FOR PEANUTS

```
  L F L W C A E N           A       S
N O T H E O R E N V E I   C A U L I F
  O N P R I R O U I A N C O U R A A E
    C O L N C K M L V A T E W O I U A
    E A E A H A F F M E N T S A A B R S I T
    A O B P R N E O T N P I H K K N D T O A C H H A P E T K
    A E G E C E L R R T O A E C E E F O P F T A K T E R D U K H P T O P D E
      P T R H E T E A P C E R L F S U P A R R I U E A E L N C A U O W O K T R A A I O
      I C F A T A S Y S E C D G P N T P A O K A S L U S O E F H T A P L H A Y P F P K
      Y A O O R E A Y T P A A M E H K E A A H E F K I W N S R H Y A A A I A R O T L
      C U I F P O M W O E F N K N H E T O N A S P I Y F E I E T N A T E W E E L I T
        L N W T U P O W R Y R U B H T U E U D S O O N G L P U I A S H A T S A M T A
        I A A A T C O H F U O L T A B H Y S N S U R N E R O S R T E R T N E T H O T
        T T K L M S Y I G G O F F S L R G K L R M A S O K A W H Y O M A S L S T L A
          E E B C P S M L N O Y G L R I A U O U R E O A E E E E T O E A I T A R O
          A E R A I P O T T I R S S C S O N O O P F L P L W T C R B A P C T T R R
          T E B I F T O L O N R N I M H I R D R I F O L A C O T E E S B O P L H P
          R C N A G P A A T N E B M D O A N G S H W A Y T D E H L R A P O P O I W
            O G F S S I L M N H B A N L A K I O T T T T E H T O E E H R C A E A O
            O H B S A R C T F E U S V S R N P E C H T H W L E V S C O A A I N R R
            E O R A C D A E A A M T E L T O K K E R T I L R O C U A O F N W N D K
            Y M I L R L E T E A T L L H C I W C T S H I D Y O O O S E T F N U I F
              M N T O C V R I A P E E I L T O E P E P E R R C H C F H S C I C T O
              R G M D A F E K P S P T M E O E E H S E C U S A I T E F Y L C S S A
              K W F A A K C A L U I N B K H E A G T K A L U T E S O E E P O B H
                O S P M N E W D E N N I N K L N A H A A A S E K H R P P E B E
                E I F T R S D K N O E R Y U I A I E I N F H Y H P I M I H E
                E L E A B I T H A C V A N     N
                O A P N N C K   R I D         A
                L M C G P     U   A           B
            Y A O O     C B M P E A P   E L   P
          A A C       T A B N L K R I T H P W O Y B
      R E F         T K P L W P N N C R Y O V N T L C T T
    A B             O A E N P K E N B L T P P A Y E S A R O N O W
    E R               S T A O E I W E K A C N A P A S A T A L F A E L T O F O E
    L I               P N U G R N Y S A L T O F M O S P B T E E I S A H A P P B R I L
        I V C O O L A S A C U C U M B E R K N O W M A L C A S A Y P P A H O N S E S
    C F K N O           F L A E E U A I E E N S Y P U S I A P W A K E U P A N C L O
  E T H A R                               T   P I E H A P P P A B U W A K E U P K N P
T E P I O                                                                       A A C P I
O L I K E                                                                     Y D S I M C
E N N A A                                                                   N A F P N E O
  W O R                                                                     R A A I H T
                                                                            O N O N A
                                                                            I E A A P
                                                                              A F I
```

Answers on page 188.

Cross-Country Maze

PLANNING

SPATIAL REASONING

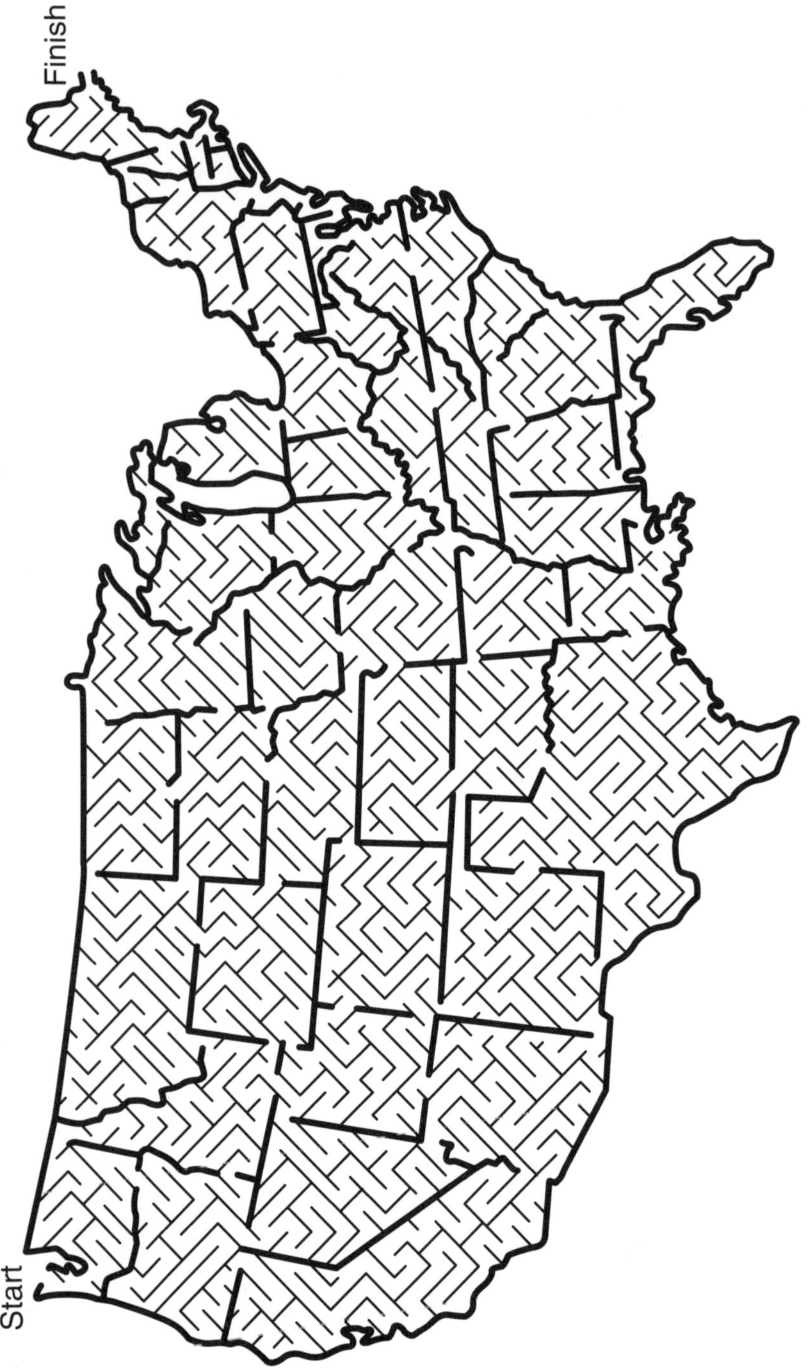

Answer on page 188.

Level 5

Waste Not, Want Not

LANGUAGE **PLANNING**

Change just one letter on each line to go from the top word to the bottom word. Do not change the order of the letters. You must have a word at each step.

HOARD

BOARD

BEARD

HEARD

____

____

____

____

____

SPEND

How Is Your Brain Like a Muscle?

New research shows that, as with muscles, the more you use a part of your brain, the larger it will become. For example, London taxi drivers have very large hippocampi—the part of the brain that deals with spatial mapping.

Also like muscles, as you use a particular part of your brain, more blood is pumped to that area to provide energy. Finally, as with muscles, the more you use your brain, the better it works.

Answers on page 188.

Card Trick

COMPUTATION LOGIC

Some cards with digits are placed to make a 3×3 grid of numbers. The current total of the numbers seen in each row and column is given. Move only 2 cards to make all the totals the same.

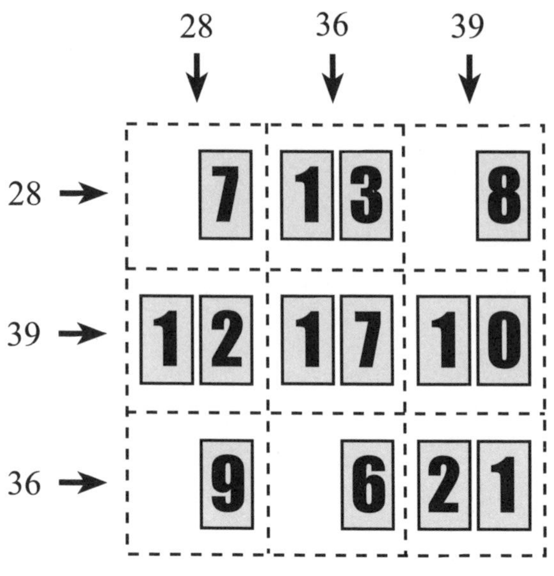

Tamagram

LANGUAGE PERCEPTION

Find an expression to define the picture below, then rearrange its letters to form a 9-letter word. LLL, for example, is THREE L's, which is an anagram for SHELTER.

Answers on pages 188–189.

Crypto-Botany

LANGUAGE LOGIC

Cryptograms are messages in substitution code. Break the code to read the message. For example, THE SMART CAT might become FVO QWGDF JGF if F is substituted for T, V for H, O for E, and so on.

Hint: In this cryptogram, the letter O stands for A.

MVHHIRAD EHOBFC (name of plant)

MVHHIRAD EHOBFC OBH LVI-JOCERLAHI CHAFRPHAFOV JOGLBRFHC. FEHN EOGH KARSKH EHOBF-CEOTHI JVLXHBC XRFE FHOBIBLT-CEOTHI, TBLFBKIRAD THFOVC, XERZE POUHC F EHP VLLU OC RJ FEHN OBH MVHHIRAD.

I Can't Feel a Thing!

There are no pain receptors in your brain. This is why doctors are able to perform brain surgery on patients who are awake.

Answers on page 189.

Frequent Flier

GENERAL KNOWLEDGE | LANGUAGE

Across

1. Chess win
5. Oodles
10. Does sums
14. Aid in crime
15. Playwright Edward
16. Robert Frost work, e.g.
17. Printed matter
18. Tribute with friendly insults
19. Preminger or Klemperer
20. Severe shocks
22. When fewer people are online, e.g.
24. Surgery sites (abbr.)
25. Sluggishness
27. What a polygraph test may reveal
28. Furnish food
30. What trick-or-treaters push
32. ___-jerk reaction
33. "My Big Fat Greek Wedding" actress Vardalos
34. Suffix with profit or racket
35. Frequent flier?
41. Response to "Are you?"
42. Owl's cry
43. Is unable to
44. Spot
48. Caterpillar or grub
49. Fuss and bother
50. Get really close
52. German article
53. Minuteman's enemy
55. A con artist pulls this
57. Tickled-pink feeling
58. They make trumpets less loud
60. Grandson of Adam
61. Pipe elbows
62. Wipe away
63. Thompson of "The Remains of the Day"
64. Take a load off
65. Groups that broke away
66. Bird abode

Down

1. Digging tools similar to pickaxes
2. Different from normal
3. Oil, in "The Ballad of Jed Clampett"
4. "___, Brute?"
5. Plastic-wrap brand
6. Neared, with "on"
7. Lawyers' grp.
8. Spaniard who explored the Mississippi
9. Ignite
10. Each, in pricing
11. "This I gotta hear!"
12. Minor point
13. Prepares ham
21. Former Russian orbiter
23. Name on a pencil
26. Driver who won't let you pass

29. Causing goosebumps
31. Kane of "All My Children"
33. Get specific about people
36. Final word
37. Folk music gathering, e.g.
38. "So sorry"
39. Makes poisonous
40. Eyes rudely
44. ___-than-life
45. "Let's Eat Right to Keep Fit" author Davis
46. Sings in the Alps, perhaps
47. Junction with surgeon's stitches
48. Bandleader Brown
51. Operates with a beam
54. "___ la vie"
56. Last year's twelve-year-old
59. Tic-___-toe

Answers on page 189.

A Startling Word Puzzle

LANGUAGE

What common English word can you think of that's 9 letters long and forms a new word every time you remove 1 letter from it? And what are the 9 common English words you can form in this way? Think about it! The answer is startling.

Fruitcake?

alchemist?

STRINGIER?

Can You Repeat that Number One More Time?

Your memory can be divided into 3 categories: long-term memory, sensory memory, and short-term memory. Short-term memory refers to memories that last for just a few minutes. Your short-term memory has a limited capacity; it can only hold about 5 to 7 items (digits, words, letters) at one time. Once short-term memory items exceed this limit, new items you try to remember will begin to "shove out" older memories. So keep a pen handy, because your short-term memory can only remember that phone number for so long!

Answers on page 189.

Word Jigsaw

SPATIAL PLANNING

Fit the pieces into the frame to form common, uncapitalized words reading across and down crossword-style. There's no need to rotate the pieces; they'll fit as shown, with each piece used exactly once.

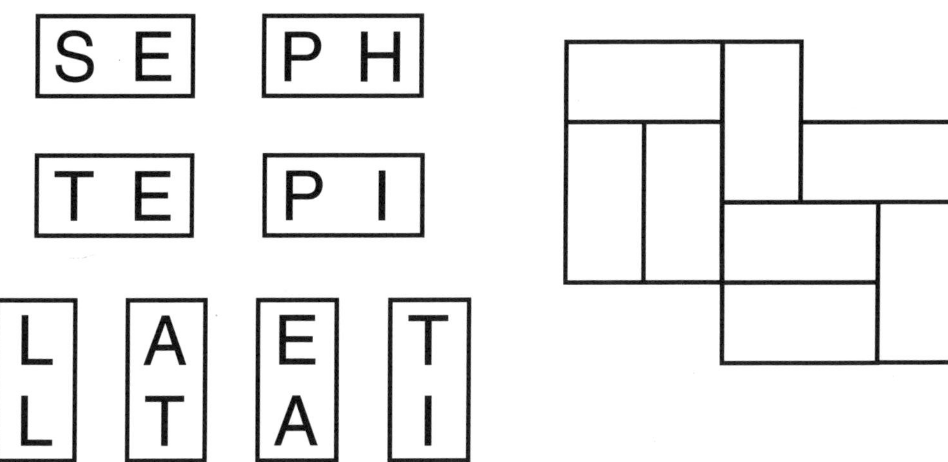

Geometric Shapes

LOGIC

SPATIAL REASONING

Divide the whole grid into smaller geometric shapes by drawing straight lines that follow either the full grid lines or the full diagonals of the square cells. Each formed shape must have exactly one symbol inside, which represents it but might not be identical to it. When the puzzle is solved, all of the grid will be used.

Hint: Each trapezoid has two sides parallel, but its other two sides are not parallel.

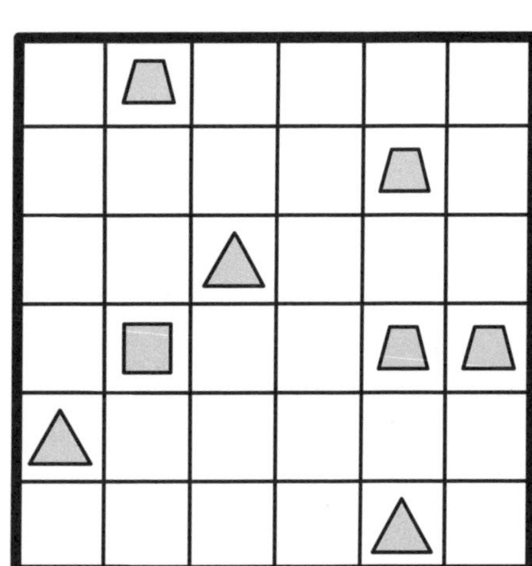

Answers on page 189.

Loop the Loops Maze

PLANNING

SPATIAL REASONING

Answer on page 189.

Add It Up

COMPUTATION LOGIC

Fill in the empty squares with numbers 1 through 9. The numbers in each row must add up to the totals in the right-hand column. The numbers in each column must add up to the totals on the bottom line. The numbers in each corner-to-corner diagonal must add up to the totals in the upper and lower right corners.

										63
	5	8	3	2	2		5	1	8	47
1		5	3	2	1	6	5	8		42
	3		2	1	6	5	8	1	2	39
1	6	2		8		7	4	9	5	46
9	1	4	3	1		1		3	9	38
5	5	9	1		5	4	6		7	53
8		6	9	4	6	2	8		2	62
6	2			7	4	7	7	1	8	46
7	7	2	5		8		2	3	7	47
4	3	8	4	2	4	1		5		44
55	42	49	36	36	42	42	51	45	66	43

The Missing Numbers

ANALYSIS CREATIVE THINKING

Each of these sequences of numbers follows a logical progression. What are the missing numbers?

A. 2, 5, ___, 11, 14

B. 10, 5, 12, ___, 14, ___, 16, 8

C. 2, 4, 8, ___, 32

D. 3, 5, 6, 8, 9, 11, ___

E. 28, 23, 19, 16, ___, 13

Answers on page 189.

Concert in the Park

ATTENTION

We count 22 things wrong with this picture. How many can you find?

Answers on page 190.

Cube Conundrum

SPATIAL VISUALIZATION

This 3-dimensional figure is made of 13 identical cubes fused together (2 cubes are hidden from view—there are 2 stacks of 3 cubes). Beneath it are 5 depictions of what the figure might look like when viewed head-on from different directions. Two of the depictions are impossible. See if you can identify them.

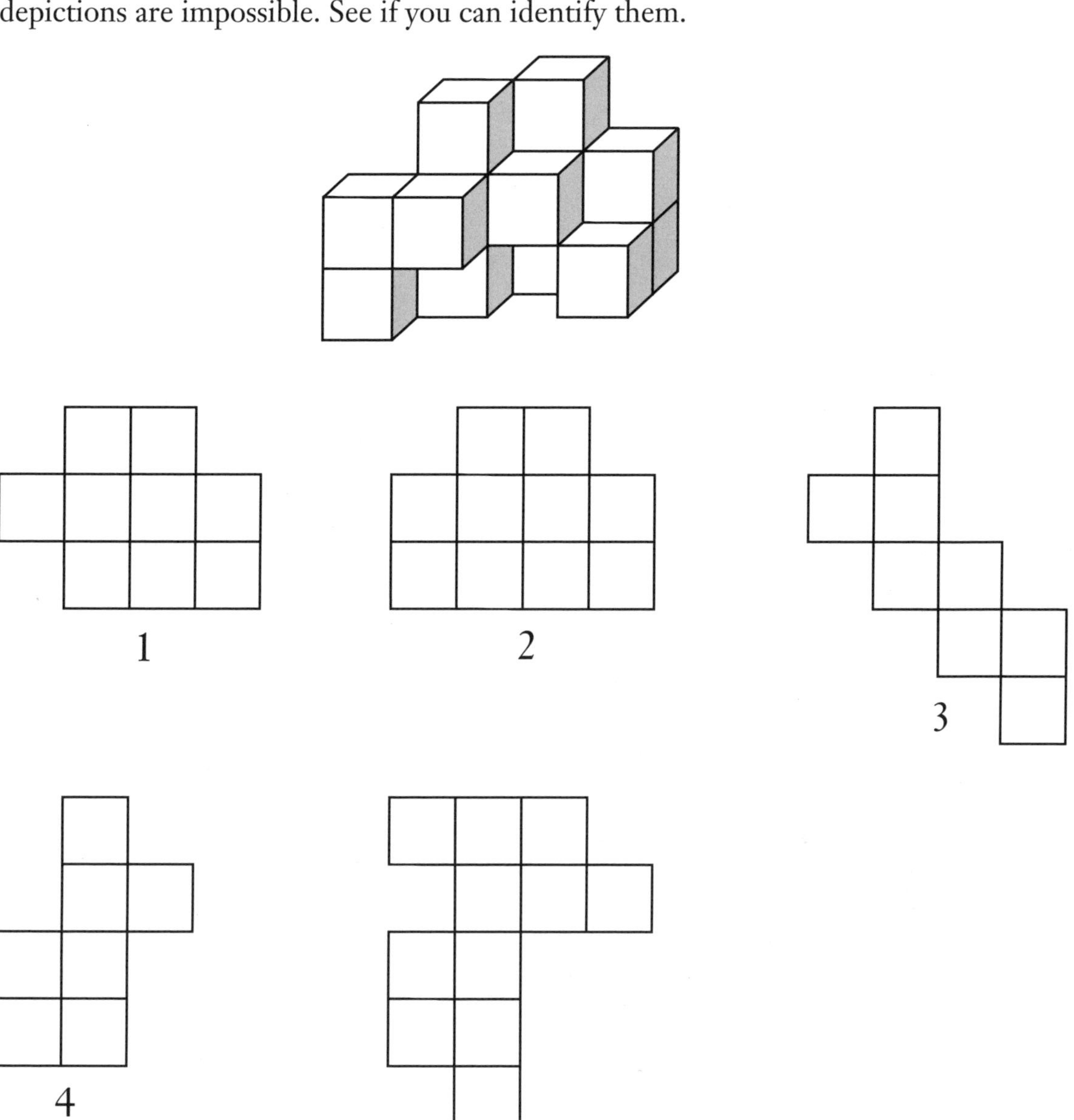

Answers on page 190.

On the Flip Side

SPATIAL VISUALIZATION

There's no trick here, only a challenge: Draw the mirror image of each of these familiar objects. You may find it harder than you think!

Grid Computing

COMPUTATION LOGIC

Each letter represents a different number from 1 through 9. Use the clues to help you put the numbers in their correct places in the grid.

A	B	C
D	E	F
G	H	J

A × H = B × F

H + D = B

D + B = F

B + F = C

B + E = J

Alphabet Jigsaw

SPATIAL REASONING

Using just your eyes, twist and turn the pieces to assemble a letter of the alphabet.

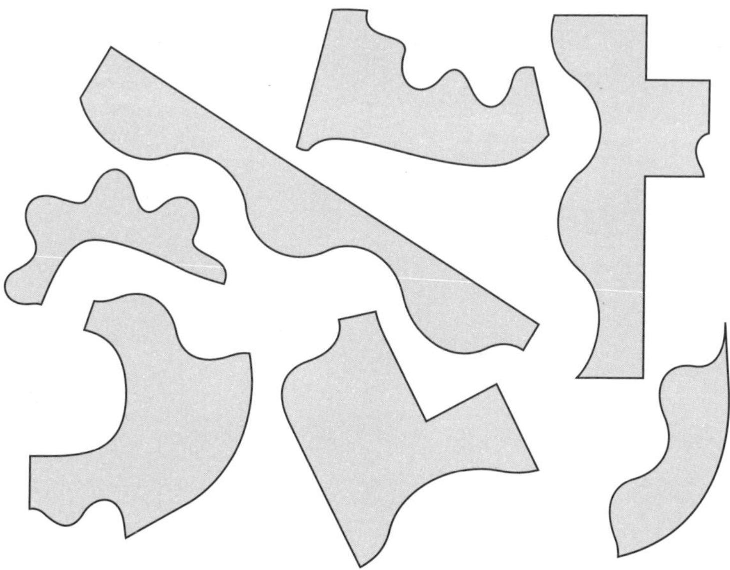

Answers on page 190.

Head Turners

ATTENTION LANGUAGE VISUAL SEARCH

Every phrase listed is contained within the box of letters. They can be found horizontally, vertically, or diagonally. They may read either backward or forward. As an added challenge, see if you can discover the theme behind the clues.

CRAM ANTONY
DOOM RING
EROS LOSER
ETON BOOK
THE FIRST LEON
FLOG CLUBS
LIAR FENCE
LIVE TWIN
LOOP HALL
LOOT BELT
NIPS THE BOTTLE
PAR SINGER
PETS ASIDE
POOH SKIRT
POTS SIGN
TOPS REMOVER
TRAP-TIME JOB
WARD LOTS
ZEUS CANAL

Theme:________________________________

```
          E V L L E R B
        Y R I W F O O D Y
      N A Y V E L A J O N E N X
      P I E R O V E R O T O R E
    S S T P G E M O T D E B P I O
  N S W I C S I G N M L L E E N W H
  I I C L E T T A N T E T O P L E H
  N T U E P T M H S I S R O T C T H
  E B L A R A O R E A S O S N S L O
  S N R A R O I N S B H R E P O P G
  E T G C N F S I B S O F A O O N N
  I N G I E A D L K O R T P P I T W
    O R H S E C I O A O H T R D I
      T S S S R S I S A K M L P
      E L L T T L U L E O E D E
        B A C O L E O R K
          W A R P D Z D
```

Answers on page 190.

Tamagram

LANGUAGE

Find an expression to define the picture shown here, then rearrange the letters of that expression to form a 10-letter word. LLL, for example, is THREE L'S, which transforms to SHELTER.

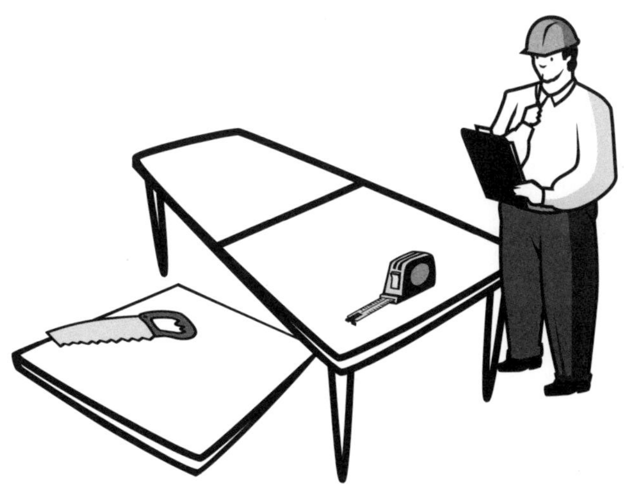

Triangle Trial

ATTENTION

How many triangles of any size are in the figure below?

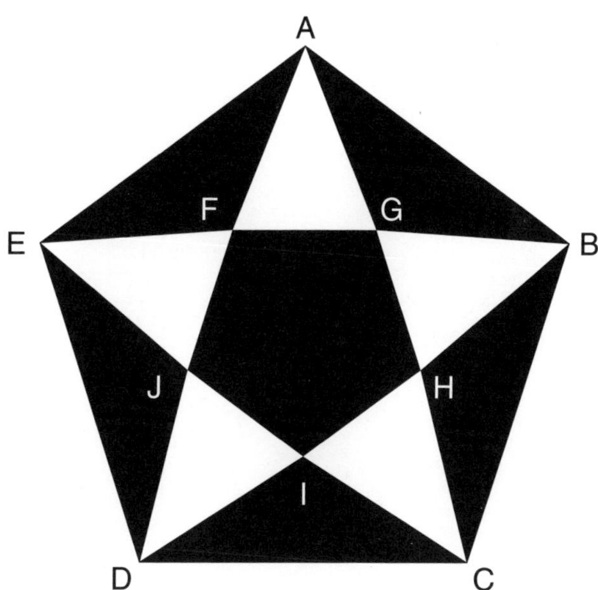

Answers on page 190.

Island Survivors

ATTENTION

There are 31 differences between the top and bottom island scenes. Can you spot all of them?

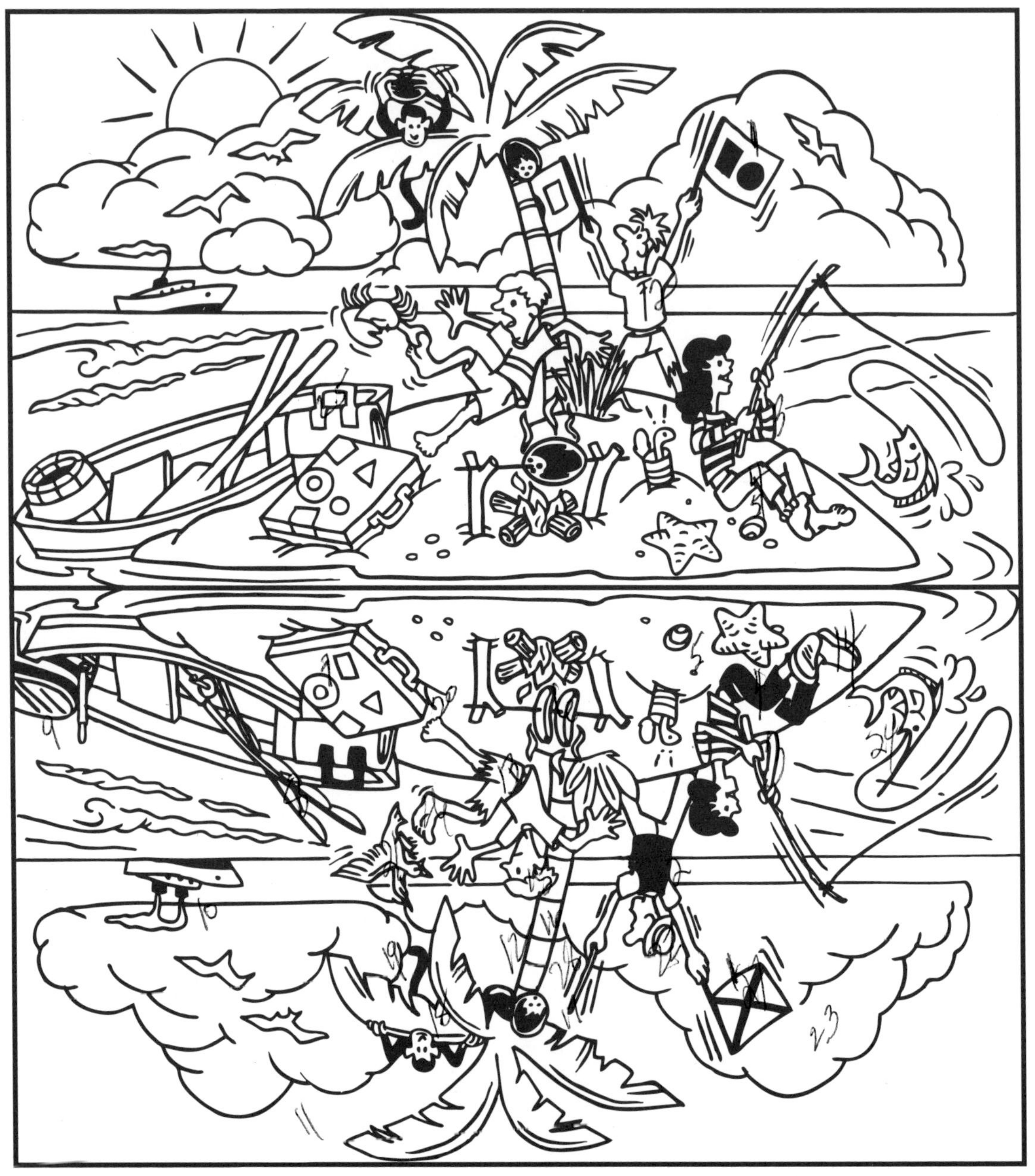

Answers on page 190.

REASSESS YOUR BRAIN

You have just completed a set of puzzles designed to challenge your various mental skills. We hope you enjoyed them. Did this mental exercise also improve your memory, attention, problem solving, and other important cognitive skills? To get a sense of your improvement, please fill out this questionnaire. It is exactly the same as the one you filled out before you worked the puzzles in this book. So now you can compare your cognitive skills before and after you embarked on a *Brain Games*® workout.

The questions below are designed to test your skills in the areas of memory, problem solving, creative thinking, attention, language, and more. Please reflect on each question, and rate your abilities on a 5-point scale, where 5 equals "excellent" and 1 equals "very poor." Then tally up your scores, and check out the categories at the bottom of the next page to learn how you have sharpened your brain.

1. When you leave your car in a large parking lot for a few hours, how good are you at remembering where you parked? Deduct points if you have to press the remote panic button and listen for the alarm to find your car.

   1 2 3 4 5

2. You have to run ten errands at different stores in the same shopping mall. How good are you at planning your trip so that you don't end up criss-crossing the mall several times before you get everything you need?

   1 2 3 4 5

3. You've got a busy day at work scheduled, but at the last minute your cat gets sick and you have to take it to the vet. How good are you at juggling your work to accommodate this unanticipated change?

   1 2 3 4 5

4. You see an ad in the morning for a new television show that's on the next evening. How likely are you to remember to watch the show?

   1 2 3 4 5

5. You're trying to work on an important project, and your coworkers are having a loud meeting next door. How well are you able to block out the distraction to concentrate on the task at hand?

   1 2 3 4 5

6. How would you rate your language skills? Are you usually able to find the right words to express a thought or idea?

   1 2 3 4 5

7. At your birthday party, you receive gifts from five different guests. If you don't write down which gift came from which guest, how likely are you to remember whom to thank for what present at the end of the night?

   1 2 3 4 5

8. How well are you able to do simple math in your head? For example, if you knew a room's dimensions, could you figure out how many yards of carpet to buy?

   1 2 3 4 5

9. How good are you at multitasking? Can you, for example, simultaneously balance your checkbook, watch the news, and talk to your spouse—and devote enough attention to each?

   1 2 3 4 5

10. When faced with important and complex issues, such as choosing an insurance plan, how good are you at using logic to determine the best option for you?

    1 2 3 4 5

10–25 Points:
Are You Ready to Make a Change?

Remember, it's never too late to improve your brain health! A great way to start is to work puzzles on a regular basis, and you've taken the first step by picking up this book. Choose a different type of puzzle each day, or do a variety of them daily to help strengthen memory, focus attention, and improve logic and problem solving.

26–40 Points:
Building Your Mental Muscle

You're no mental slouch, but there's always room to sharpen your mind! Choose puzzles that will challenge you, especially the types of puzzles you might not like as much or would normally avoid. Remember, doing a puzzle can be the mental equivalent of doing lunges or squats: While they might not be your first choice of activity, you'll definitely like the results!

41–50 Points:
View from the Top

Congratulations! You're keeping your brain in tip-top shape. To maintain this level of mental fitness, keep challenging yourself by working puzzles every day. Like the rest of the body's muscles, your mental strength can decline if you don't use it. So choose to keep your brain strong and active. You're at the summit—now you just have to stay to enjoy the view!

ANSWERS

Max and Mitch (page 11)

1. C. ELECTRIC GUITAR
2. D. SAXOPHONE
3. F. DRUM MAJORETTE
4. B. TAMBOURINE
5. E. HARMONICA
6. A. ACCORDION

Aptagrams (page 11)

1. dormitory; 2. clothespins; 3. the Hilton; 4. Barbie doll

How Long Does It Take? (page 12)

1. To see a three-ring circus: two to three hours.
2. A balloon to pop: two-thousandths of a second.
3. A blue shark to swim a mile: one minute and forty-three seconds.
4. A cloud to recharge after lightning flashes: twenty seconds.
5. A day to pass on Neptune compared to an Earth day: sixteen hours.

Look Before You . . . (page 13)

LEAP, heap, hemp, hump, JUMP

Layer by Layer (page 13)

One possibility is shown below. You may have found others.

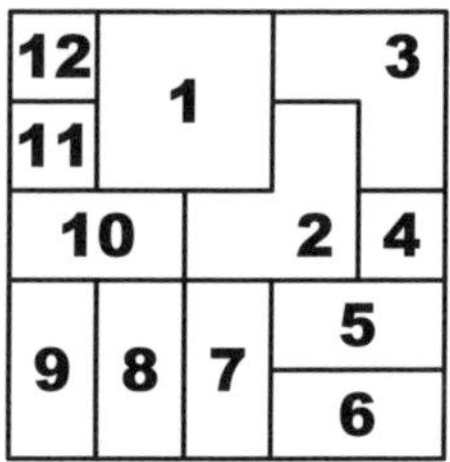

Profit in Baskets (pages 14–15)

Retinue of R's (page 16)

1. rabbit; 2. radish; 3. rag; 4. railing; 5. rain barrel; 6. rain gutter; 7. rain spout; 8. road; 9. robot; 10. rock; 11. rocking chair; 12. roof; 13. rose

Playing the Market (page 16)

When he bought the stock, Steve was a billionaire.

Fitting Words (page 17)

P	A	R	I	S
E	R	O	D	E
A	C	T	O	R
S	H	E	L	F

Sudoku (page 17)

2	6	8	3	5	9	4	1	7
4	3	5	1	6	7	9	2	8
7	1	9	8	4	2	5	3	6
6	9	2	7	8	1	3	5	4
8	5	1	4	2	3	6	7	9
3	7	4	6	9	5	2	8	1
5	4	3	9	1	8	7	6	2
1	2	6	5	7	4	8	9	3
9	8	7	2	3	6	1	4	5

Answers

Geometric Shapes (page 18)

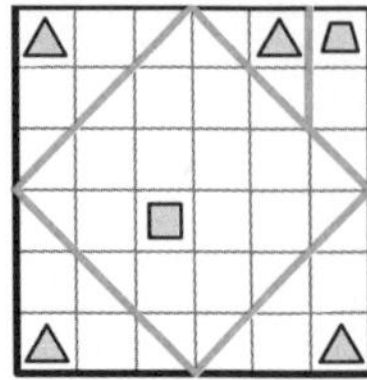

Rhyme Time (page 18)

1. fax tax; 2. try rye; 3. new crew; 4. sold gold; 5. good wood; 6. dark mark; 7. heat meat; 8. great mate; 9. richer pitcher; 10. pleasant pheasant

Soupy Sailfish (page 19)

Cone You Top This? (pages 20–21)

V T E N T O I G
A K X R Z U W P A D G L
X N A T A E S G L Z A A B T
P G O Y D I R N E A K Y R U S U
U N I A T L I O O Y K L D R Y D
G I T K J E F W B G S I E N O M
P N P A I O R P C B R P G N I V I D
O I M C N E M M O T O R H O M E E T
O B A A G L O A N U U I T Z G R K H
A L U C V Y C T C E B N N Z R U R A T O
T T T L I A W M R D K I S O M D
B B D N S E A O R C L I W M I P
S G G O P H T W P L E D O C G P
W N A O A E I Q L R C N N L
I I P R R N O A K I I B
N M T S K Y B C E T
G M K C J E E U
N X I G E S G C
I K I W T A N E
L L N H S B I B
I S G B K Y K R
A I M J I N I A
S G O D T O H B
G N I T F A R B
J E P N V M R B

Where Are the Animals? (page 23)

1. dog/cat; 2. skunk/elk; 3. deer/owl; 4. fox/snake; 5. wolf/horse; 6. rabbit/elephant; 7. tiger/lion; 8. monkey/eagle; 9. seal/whale; 10. parrot/eel

The Shading Game (page 24)

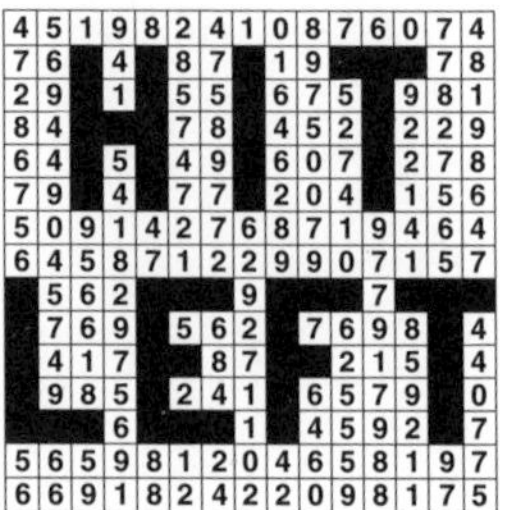

Many Mice (page 25)

5: TaMI CEntered the ceraMIC Egg that Mick eventually gave her so she wouldn't miss him while he worked for the AtoMIC Energy commission. Tami smoothed the egg with a puMICE stone, the only one in her domicile. Tami enjoyed the egg, but Mick's gift of an imported salaMI CEmented their relationship and helped her to miss him less.

It's Tricky!, Part II (page 26)

The items that don't belong to Jocko are the 4 linked rings (Jocko has 3), the gloves with the stars (Jocko's are white), and the cage with the gorilla (Jocko has a tiger).

Crypto-Wisdom (page 26)

1. A rolling stone gathers no moss.
2. A penny saved is a penny earned.
3. Kind words linger in the heart.

Read Between the Lines (page 27)

1. a) mammoth, b) man, c) manacle
2. a) rumpus, b) run, c) runaway
3. a) manuscript, b) many, c) map
4. a) riser, b) risk, c) risqué
5. a) sister, b) sit, c) sitar

"A man sits as many risks as he runs."
—Henry David Thoreau

Flying High (page 28)

COANFL	FALCON
RIOBN	ROBIN
CAALINRD	CARDINAL
NAARYC	CANARY
BIRDULEB	BLUEBIRD
WOCR	CROW
EGLAE	EAGLE
WSROPRA	SPARROW
GASLIRNT	STARLING

FREE AS A BIRD
1 2 3 4 5 6 7 8 9 10 11

Assemblage of A's (page 29)

1. aardvark; 2. abacus; 3. airplane; 4. alcove; 5. ankles; 6. apple; 7. archer; 8. arch; 9. argyle socks, 10. armor; 11. arms; 12. arrow; 13. artichoke; 14. astronaut; 15. ax

Rectangle Census (page 29)

There are 12 rectangles. Using the lettered diagram below, they are: ABH, BCD, DEF, FGH, B, D, F, H, J, DE, EF, EJ

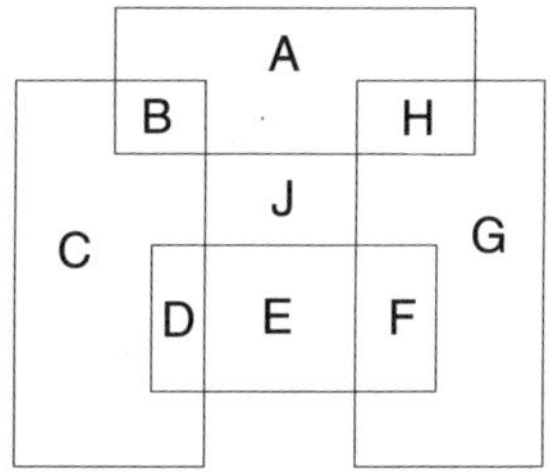

You Auto Like This (pages 30–31)

Cheer Up! (page 32)

Answers may vary.
SAD, sod, soy, JOY

Word Jigsaw (page 32)

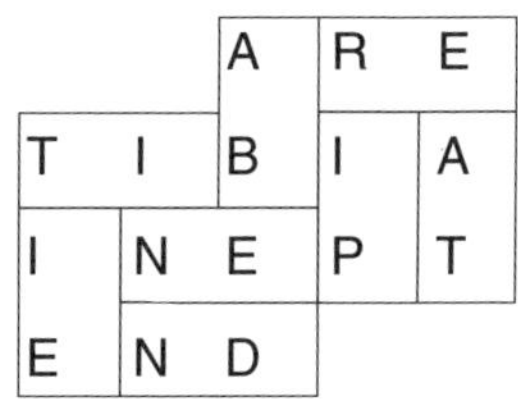

Fish Fantasy (page 33)

Max and Mitch Strike Again (page 34)

1. D. SMILEY FACE
2. C. GONDOLA
3. A. CHAMELEON
4. D. OLD GLORY

Geometric Shapes (page 34)

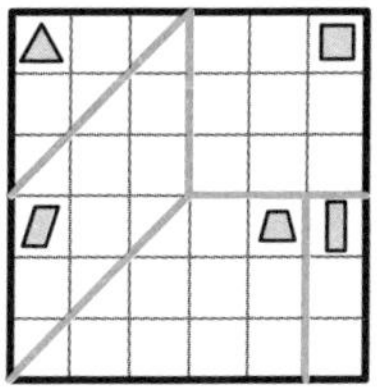

Answers

Continuous Line Bet (page 35)

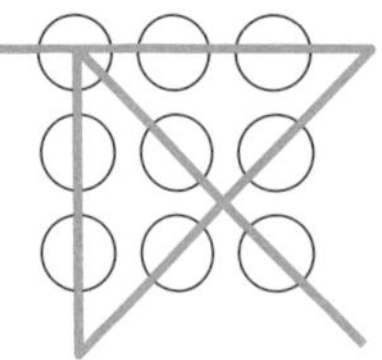

Honeycomb (page 35)

Fitting Words (page 37)

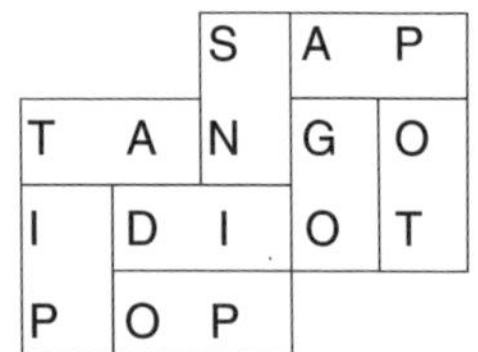

Word Jigsaw (page 37)

Let's Get Away from It All (pages 38–39)

Rhyme Time (page 40)

1. lox box; 2. feed seed; 3. darn barn; 4. main pain; 5. gold mold; 6. squid bid; 7. swell smell; 8. vault fault; 9. small shawl; 10. rehearse verse

No Buts About It! (page 40)

15: Bob, a bubba from Old KnoB, UTah, stole BUTter from a BUTcher and was sentenced to jail. "I made a booboo," BoB UTtered to the judge, BUT the judge said, "BoB, UTica is the prison for thieves like you." "BUT, BUT!" stammered Tab, underpaid attorney for BoB. "UTica is bad for BUTter thieves." "No ifs, ands, or BUTs," reBUTted the judge. "BoB, UTica awaits your deBUT as a prisoner tomorrow." Bob, turning to his beautiful gal BaB, UTtered, Buh-bye."

It's a Jungle (of Numbers!) Out There (page 41)

Rhyme Time (page 42)

1. fun run; 2. too few; 3. law flaw; 4. blue shoe; 5. neat feat; 6. make steak; 7. black snack; 8. chief thief; 9. shore store; 10. ocean motion

The Great Escape (page 42)

The other end of the chain wasn't attached to anything.

Make a Match (page 43)

1. C. SATELLITE DISH
2. D. BUTTER DISH
3. B. FIENDISH
4. A. CHAFING DISH

XOXO (page 44)

Answer may vary.

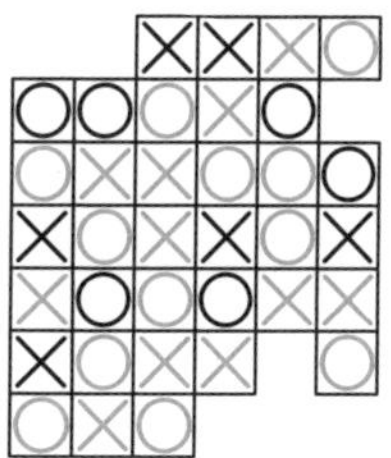

We Shall Over... Come (page 44)

OVER, ever, eves, eyes, dyes, does, dots, dote, dome, COME

Let's Make Some Music (page 45)

1	2	3	4	5	6	7	8	9	10	11	12	13
G	H	P	I	A	N	O	J	W	T	X	K	F
14	15	16	17	18	19	20	21	22	23	24	25	26
D	R	U	M	Z	L	S	B	E	C	V	Y	Q

Number Crossword (page 46)

■	■	5	1
9	9	9	9
3	4	5	6
7	6	■	■

Fitting Words (page 46)

S	T	O	L	E
P	I	X	E	L
O	M	E	N	S
T	E	N	S	E

Zone of Z's (page 47)

1. zebra; 2. zeppelin; 3. zigzag; 4. zinnia; 5. zipper; 6. zither; 7. zoot suit; 8. zucchini

Hurry! (pages 48–49)

Crazy Mixed-Up Letters (page 51)

3: hornets, shorten, thrones

Tag! You're It! (page 52)

The next letter is "M." The sequence is E, M, M, M—eeney, meeney, miney, moe.

Sudoku (page 52)

5	3	9	7	2	1	8	6	4
1	4	8	6	5	3	2	9	7
7	2	6	8	4	9	3	1	5
2	9	5	1	6	4	7	8	3
8	6	7	9	3	2	5	4	1
3	1	4	5	7	8	6	2	9
4	7	2	3	1	6	9	5	8
9	5	1	2	8	7	4	3	6
6	8	3	4	9	5	1	7	2

Circus Time (page 53)

S	S	T	S	I	L	A	I	R	E	A	R	E	I	R
T	I	G	H	T	R	O	P	E	N	G	Z	S	I	E
N	I	R	E	K	R	A	B	T	L	E	I	N	R	W
A	N	G	N	G	R	B	R	S	P	O	G	W	E	O
H	R	T	E	A	L	B	E	A	R	S	H	O	D	R
P	O	S	D	R	I	I	R	M	F	T	M	L	I	H
E	C	E	I	G	S	T	O	G	E	A	E	C	R	T
L	P	R	T	D	G	S	B	N	G	P	T	S	K	E
E	O	O	M	N	E	A	T	I	T	E	T	M	C	F
R	P	N	I	U	M	S	C	R	A	A	N	D	A	I
B	A	Y	D	L	S	S	H	I	B	N	M	L	B	N
Y	L	T	W	E	L	H	E	O	E	U	G	E	E	K
F	R	E	A	A	T	A	R	B	W	T	E	S	R	T
S	H	L	Y	O	W	C	C	O	U	S	N	E	A	A
R	S	T	Y	D	A	L	D	E	D	R	A	E	B	H

Answers

Rhyme Time (page 54)

1. meal deal; 2. free tree; 3. late date; 4. wave slave; 5. bowl goal; 6. more score; 7. loud crowd; 8. fling king; 9. dandy candy; 10. great slate; 11. champ gramp; 12. large barge; 13. blower mower; 14. cranky Yankee; 15. normal formal

See Your Name in Print! (page 55)

YOUR
NAME

Wise Words (page 55)

The next letter is "E." The sequence is A, P, S, I, A, P, E—a penny saved is a penny earned.

Bugs in the System (page 56)

Find It!, Part I (page 57)

diamond, opal, ruby; cheetah, giraffe, leopard; Toyota, Cadillac, Ferrari; Dali, Matisse, Picasso

C H S A D Q T W F Z Q
M A F E R R A R I S J
A T D N O M A I D G F
T E A I I L A P O T G
I E L Q L T O Y O T A
S H I W N L F W Y E M
S C V E F F A R I G L
E C R O S S A C I P B
Z L R U B Y T Z Q E T

Find It!, Part II (page 58)

10: giraffe, Toyota, diamond, Ferrari, cheetah, Picasso, opal, ruby, Cadillac, Matisse

Anagrams in the Abstract (page 58)

1. C. EMPATHY
2. E. MEMORY
3. B. PHILOSOPHY
4. A. CREATIVITY
5. F. LIBERTY
6. D. ROMANCE

Made Ya Laugh! (page 59)

1. "Why do they call it a 'building?' It looks like it's finished. Why isn't it a 'built?' "

—Jerry Seinfeld

2. A Freudian slip is when you say one thing but mean your mother.
3. Her vocabulary was as bad as, like, whatever.
4. "I planted some bird seed. A bird grew. Now I don't know what to feed it."

—Steven Wright

5. Where do forest rangers go to get away from it all?

Why Can't We Make Just One? (page 60)

The word is AMENDS. It's a quirk of language that you never hear of anyone making an amend.

Why Worry? (page 60)

Let It Be

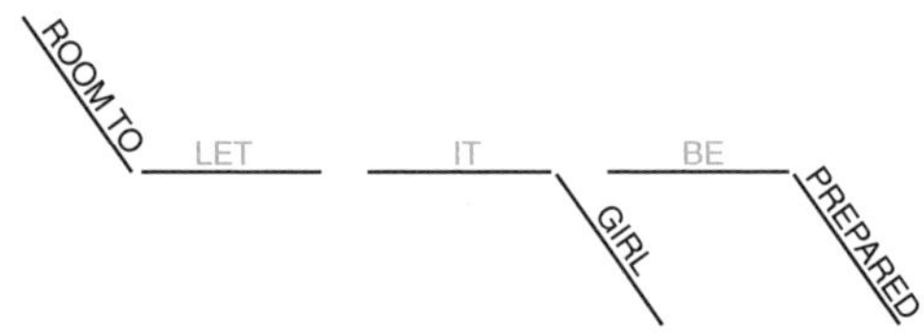

Sudoku (page 61)

1	6	2	5	3	8	7	9	4
4	7	8	2	6	9	5	1	3
5	3	9	7	1	4	2	8	6
2	8	3	1	7	6	9	4	5
7	4	1	9	5	3	8	6	2
9	5	6	4	8	2	1	3	7
8	9	7	6	4	5	3	2	1
3	1	4	8	2	7	6	5	9
6	2	5	3	9	1	4	7	8

Word Jigsaw (page 61)

B	R	A		
O	O	M	P	H
A	D	I	E	U
		D	A	M

Geometric Shapes (page 62)

Count the Shapes (page 62)

There are 6 squares.

It All Adds Up (page 63)

				18
4	8	7	5	24
3	7	6	4	20
2	6	5	3	16
1	5	4	2	12
10	26	22	14	18

Totally Cubular! (page 63)

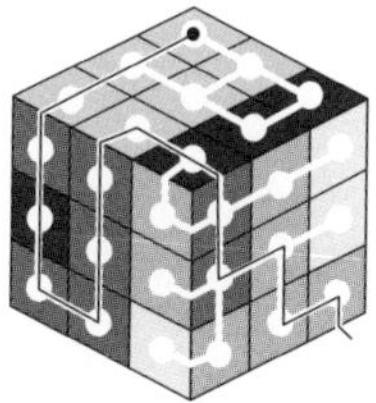

Checkerboard Puzzle (page 64)

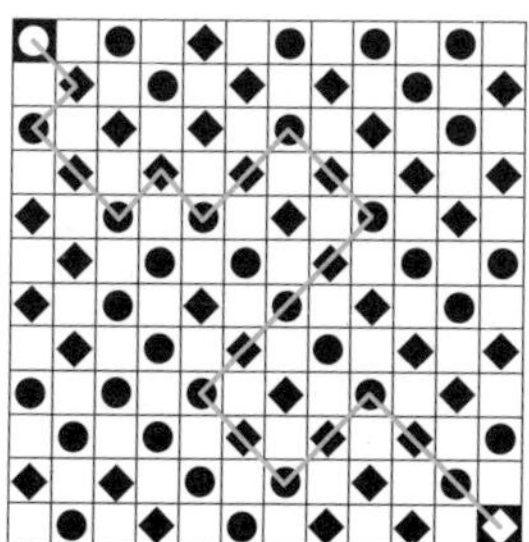

December the What? (page 65)

The date is Sunday, December 13:

Clue 1 eliminates December 5, 10, 15, 20, 25, and 30.

Clue 2 eliminates December 24 and 31.

Clue 3 eliminates December 1, 2, 3, 4, 6, 7, 8, 9, 11, 12, 22, and 23.

Clue 4 eliminates December 16, 17, 18, 19, 26, 27, 28, and 29.

Clue 5 eliminates December 14 and 21.

Geometric Cube Construction (page 66)

Answer is C.

Fitting Words (page 67)

R	A	T	T	Y
I	N	U	R	E
D	E	B	I	T
S	W	A	M	I

Geometric Shapes (page 67)

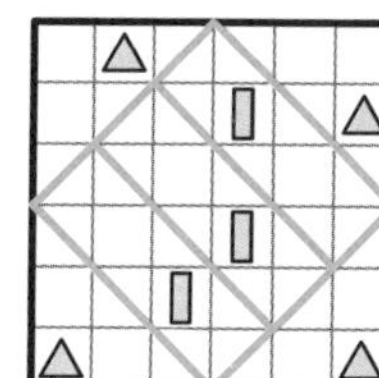

Stop and Smell the Flowers (page 68)

1	2	3	4	5	6	7	8	9	10	11	12	13
X	J	C	V	I	O	L	E	T	F	Q	G	U
14	15	16	17	18	19	20	21	22	23	24	25	26
Z	W	R	M	K	D	P	A	N	S	Y	B	H

Batteries Not Included (page 69)

1. Some assembly required.
2. Use only as directed.
3. As seen on TV.
4. Avoid contact with skin.
5. Apply only to affected area.
6. You must be present to win.
7. Harmful or fatal if swallowed.
8. No purchase necessary!

Answers

Presidential Puzzle (pages 70–71)

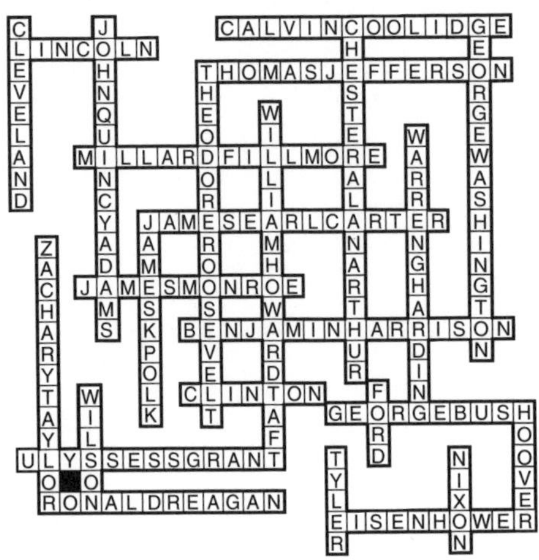

Circle Takes the Square (page 72)

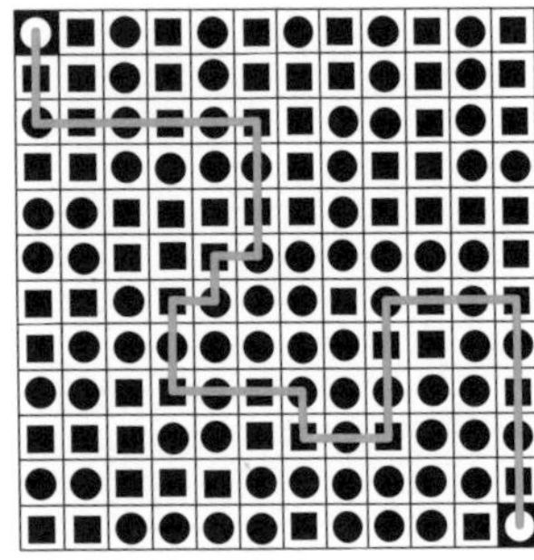

Barbershop Duet (page 73)

1. three men in the mirror; 2. customer has hair in the mirror; 3. person on coatrack; 4. magazine is upside-down, 5. sandwich on price list; 6. everyone is bald; 7. shampoo costs more than a haircut

Word of Mouth (page 73)

T	O	H	U	M
H	U	M	T	O
M	T	O	H	U
O	H	U	M	T
U	M	T	O	H

Road Trip! (pages 74)

Famished Family (page 75)

Multiplication Table (page 76)

1	3	2	5	4
2	1	5	4	3
4	2	3	1	5
3	5	4	2	1
5	4	1	3	2

Dissection (page 76)

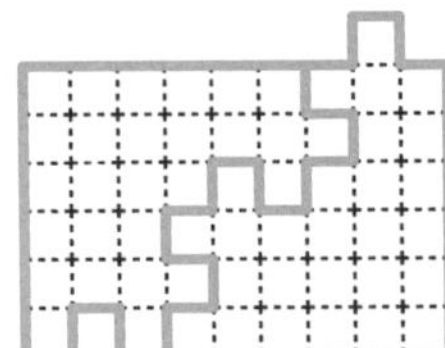

Not-So-Happy Birthday (page 77)

The date is January 1. Molly's birthday is December 31. Two days ago, on December 30 of last year, she was 39. That means today, she is 40. On December 31 of this year, she will turn 41. On December 31 of next year, she will turn 42. So next year, she really will be 42 and Homer will still be in the doghouse.

Finding a Digit (page 77)

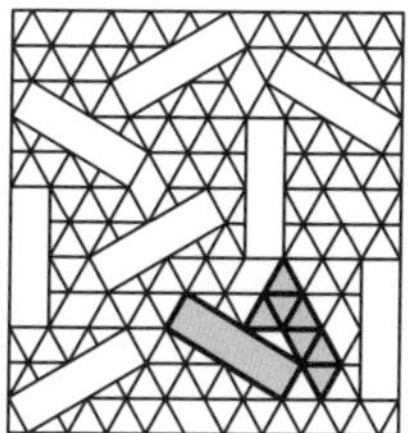

Word Columns (page 78)

A husband said to his wife, "No, I don't hate your relatives. In fact, I like your mother-in-law better than I like mine."

A husband said to his
wife, "No, I don't hate
your relatives. In fact,
I like your
mother-in-law better
than I like mine."

Another Doggone Jigsaw (page 79)

The Logic of Crayons (pages 80–81)

Sabrina likes fruits and vegetables, so her lip gloss is either Strawberry Lip Smackers or Plum Wicked. Her crayon color is either Neon Carrot or Vivid Tangerine. Kelly borrowed the Vivid Tangerine crayon, so that's not her crayon color. The Bubble Gum lip gloss isn't hers, either. The item that could remind Jill of her doll Elmo is Tickle Me Pink (a la Tickle Me Elmo), so that's a good bet for her crayon. The only lip gloss with a "seductive" and "devilish" sound is Plum Wicked, and it's also a "fruity flavor," so enter that one as Kris's lip gloss. The crayon color Mauvelous is the only one that's a shade of violet/purple, and the punny "Mauvelous" sounds like the breezy "wunnerful," so that's a lock for Kelly's crayon. Kris doesn't have pink, and she doesn't like vegetables, so she also doesn't have Neon Carrot. If she doesn't have the carrot, then Sabrina must have it, so you can plug that in for Sabrina's crayon. If Kelly likes violet shades and also "all-day" suckers, she must have the Hard Candy Lollipop lip gloss. The strawberry is the only fruit with its seeds on the outside, so Sabrina's lip gloss must be the Strawberry Smackers. By now we know three of the lip glosses, so the fourth one, by elimination, must be Bubble Gum for Jill.

Girl	Crayon Color	Lip Gloss
Sabrina	Neon Carrot	Strawberry Smackers
Jill	Tickle Me Pink	Bubble Gum
Kelly	Mauvelous	Hard Candy Lollipop
Kris	Vivid Tangerine	Plum Wicked

Sage Advice (page 82)

The missing letter is "P." The sequence is: A fool and his money are soon parted.

Let's Make Bread! (page 82)

Answers may vary.
FLOUR, floor, flood, blood, brood, broad, BREAD

Say It Again, Sam (page 83)

1. ate eight; 2. add ad; 3. pale pail; 4. peace piece; 5. pear pair; 6. pier peer; 7. plain plane; 8. whole hole; 9. wholly holy; 10. Whig wig; 11. one won; 12. whale wail; 13. vain vein; 14. toe tow; 15. write right; 16. wry rye; 17. sole soul; 18. packed pact; 19. prophet profit; 20. colonel kernel; 21. hale hail; 22. morning mourning; 23. mustered mustard; 24. complement compliment; 25. ball bawl; 26. ascent assent

Answers

Sudoku (page 85)

1	2	3	5	7	9	6	8	4
6	5	8	1	4	3	7	9	2
7	9	4	2	8	6	1	3	5
9	4	1	8	5	7	2	6	3
3	7	5	9	6	2	8	4	1
8	6	2	4	3	1	9	5	7
2	3	7	6	9	4	5	1	8
4	8	9	7	1	5	3	2	6
5	1	6	3	2	8	4	7	9

Count the Shapes (page 85)

There are 8 squares.

Layer by Layer (page 86)

One possibility is shown here. You may have found others.

Next Letter? (page 86)

"E" as in "eight." The other letters are the first letters of the numbers one through seven.

Imbroglio of I's (page 87)

1. ice cream; 2. ice-cream cone; 3. ice skates; 4. igloo; 5. iguana; 6. incandescent bulb; 7. ink bottle; 8. ionic column; 9. Irish setter; 10. iron; 11. ironing board; 12. island; 13. ivy

Misleading Sequence (page 87)

12 + 6 = 18

To the Letter (page 88)

A	B	C	D	E	F
3	5	1	2	4	7

Name Game (page 88)

LOLA appears 5 times. LULU appears 4 times. AL appears 11 times. LOU appears 16 times.

Logical Hats (page 89)

The numbers on A and C are 10 and 5. B sees these and realizes he either has 15 or 5 on his hat. He then realizes that if he had 5 on his hat, A would have seen 5 and 5 and would have known his own hat had a 10. Since A didn't know his number, B eliminates this possibility.

Fitting Words (page 89)

F	I	L	T	H
A	D	I	E	U
T	O	M	E	S
S	L	O	S	H

Find It (pages 90–91)

Erie, Huron, Ontario; oboe, piano; blue, orange, purple; Jaws, Titanic; beagle, boxer, collie, pug; Dylan, Hope

B	O	X	E	R	O	C	H	F	N
L	N	T	G	L	I	O	P	H	E
U	T	N	N	N	P	I	U	L	I
E	A	D	A	E	A	R	G	G	L
G	R	T	R	N	O	A	U	F	L
U	I	I	O	N	E	B	S	P	O
T	O	R	E	B	T	Z	O	D	C
B	D	Y	L	A	N	S	W	A	J

Easy as ABC (page 92)

D		B	C	A	
	A	C		D	B
C		D	B		A
A	B		D		C
	C		A	B	D
B	D	A		C	

Relying on Hope (page 92)

On a wing and a prayer

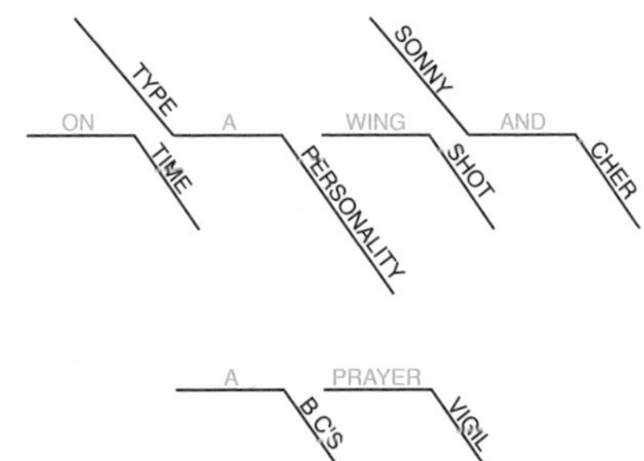

Number Crossword (page 93)

9	7	■	■
6	8	2	4
3	9	4	5
■	■	2	6

Unbearable Jigsaw (page 94)

Count the Shapes (page 95)

There are 9 squares.

Word Jigsaw 20 (page 95)

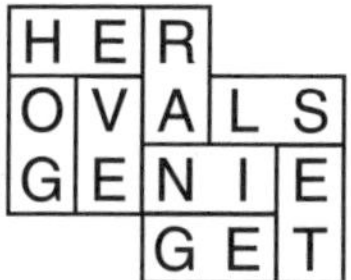

Fit It! (pages 96–97)

M	O	O	N	■	A	S	H	E	■	S	A	M
E	R	N	E	■	S	E	E	R	■	P	G	A
S	L	A	G	■	P	A	R	I	S	I	A	N
S	A	T	E	S	■	M	A	N	I	K	I	N
I	N	E	V	E	R	■	■	■	X	E	N	A
A	D	A	■	W	I	T	H	I	T	■	■	■
H	O	R	S	E	F	E	A	T	H	E	R	S
■	■	■	C	R	E	A	M	S	■	M	A	T
M	U	I	R	■	■	■	M	O	T	I	V	E
A	N	N	E	X	E	S	■	K	A	T	I	E
T	H	E	W	O	R	K	S	■	S	T	O	P
Z	I	P	■	U	N	I	T	■	T	E	L	L
O	P	T	■	T	O	N	Y	■	E	D	I	E

Number Maze (page 98)

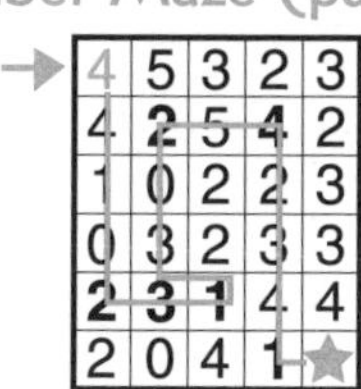

Why Walk When You Can Ride? (page 98)

WALK, wale, wide, RIDE

Anagrammatically Correct (page 99)

1. this/hits
2. toms/most
3. left/felt
4. tale/late
5. acre/race
6. sore/rose
7. cats/cast/acts
8. snap/pans/naps

Pyramid (page 99)

E
DE
DEN
REND
UNDER
ENDURE
DENTURE
VENTURED
ADVENTURE
UNTRAVELED

All That & Less (page 100)

T	O	H	E	C	O	Y	A	E	Y	I	N	K	S	E	C
N	U	N	T	I	&	V	L	B	H	&	I	E	L	E	T
T	O	E	E	D	R	Y	&	&	&	N	C	C	R	S	S
H	A	C	M	A	O	E	G	B	G	O	&	E	R	N	H
D	&	I	&	&	R	A	&	F	&	L	N	E	Y	A	H
R	J	T	N	O	R	M	E	G	E	L	&	S	I	E	S
A	E	O	O	I	C	R	E	I	A	S	E	S	H	&	V
E	C	&	D	H	D	&	N	D	L	E	S	I	L	I	S
E	K	N	X	I	&	T	I	E	B	E	K	S	X	&	P
B	I	Y	N	E	H	C	N	D	M	&	I	A	C	I	E
E	&	&	&	E	L	O	O	S	C	&	I	A	T	F	D
N	R	T	W	V	L	A	L	M	S	A	S	T	&	E	P
L	A	I	S	O	K	E	Y	U	B	T	M	A	C	E	D
B	N	Y	C	&	&	C	O	&	L	A	N	E	T	H	E
D	A	M	P	H	R	H	I	E	R	C	T	E	R	R	S
A	N	D	S	Y	T	G	S	D	E	B	M	B	O	A	L

Leftover letters spell: The consecutive letters A-N-D have been replaced by the ampersand symbol.

Sign of the Times (page 101)

3	1	3	3	**27**
1	5	5	9	**225**
7	5	5	1	**175**
7	2	1	2	**28**
147	**50**	**75**	**54**	

Answers

Number Maze (page 101)

Word Jigsaw (page 102)

		F	R	Y
V	A	L	U	E
E	D	I	T	S
T	O	P		

Ageless Logic (page 102)

Grandma is 61.

On the Plus Side (page 103)

							26
2	3	6	8	7	3	5	34
3	4	3	9	1	4	7	31
8	2	7	5	3	6	8	39
9	6	2	6	7	3	9	42
1	3	1	9	5	2	1	22
3	5	4	7	1	8	6	34
2	4	9	5	8	2	4	34
28	27	32	49	32	28	40	36

Star Power (page 104)

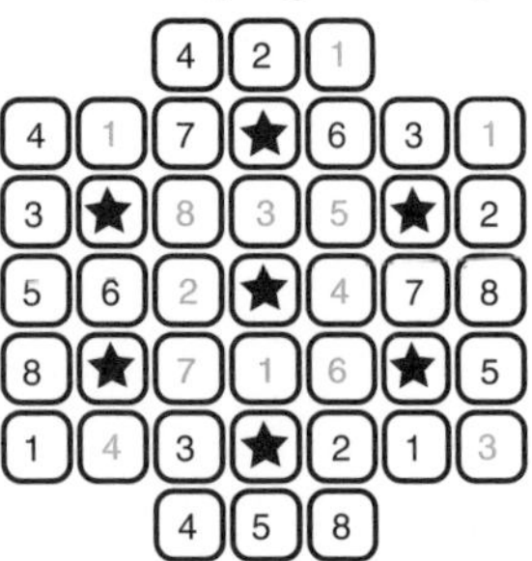

The Office (page 106)

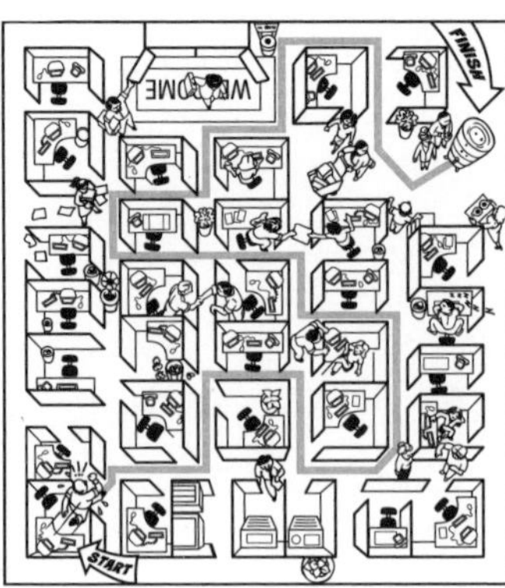

Red, White, and Blue (page 107)

	A	B	C	D	E	F
1	B	W	R	R	B	W
2	R	W	B	W	R	B
3	W	B	R	B	W	R
4	R	B	W	R	W	B
5	W	R	B	W	B	R
6	B	R	W	B	R	W

My Thoughts, Add-xactly! (page 108)

									47
1	6	4	6	9	3	6	5	4	44
7	9	8	9	3	2	1	9	2	50
6	2	2	5	1	3	5	6	3	33
5	8	9	7	9	8	4	8	7	65
1	4	8	5	3	5	2	1	9	38
9	5	6	3	2	8	9	3	1	46
3	1	7	9	7	9	4	7	8	55
6	2	8	1	2	2	8	6	4	39
6	3	6	4	7	5	7	1	5	44
44	40	58	49	43	45	46	46	43	45

From Adore to Scorn (page 109)

ADORE, adorn, acorn, SCORN

Rectangle Roundup (page 109)

There are 18 rectangles.

Find It (page 110)

azalea, carnation, marigold; crow, india ink, soot; handball, skiing, soccer; Shangri-la, El Dorado, Holy Grail; private, captain, major

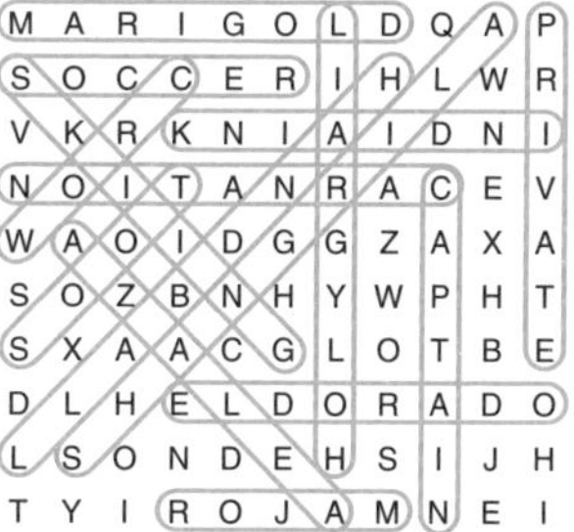

Anagram President (page 111)

1. hardy; 2. amble; 3. rumba; 4. rinse; 5. yanks; 6. tuber; 7. relay; 8. urban; 9. melon; 10. alter; 11. Nepal

President: Harry Truman

Star Power (page 112)

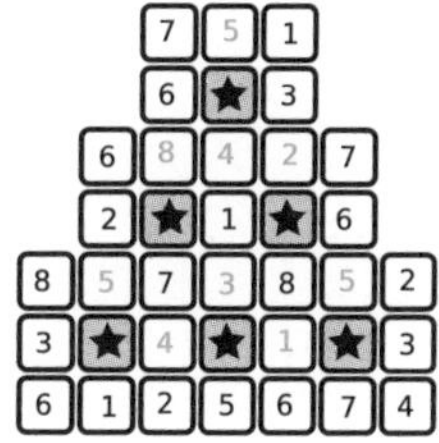

Word Paths (page 113)

1. Waste not, want not.
2. Look before you leap.
3. Practice what you preach.
4. A stitch in time saves nine.

Menagerie Nursery (pages 114–115)

Alphabet Puzzle (page 116)

A	B	C	D	E	O	I	M	N	O	P
B	G	D	E	L	M	N	O	P	U	Q
C	F	E	J	K	L	G	R	Q	T	R
D	G	H	I	N	M	Q	Q	R	S	U
E	L	I	J	O	N	O	P	Q	R	S
F	G	J	K	P	O	S	T	U	W	T
G	H	S	L	R	P	Q	R	S	V	F
J	I	N	M	N	Q	R	U	T	U	V
W	V	O	T	O	R	S	T	U	R	W
X	W	V	U	P	U	T	X	V	U	X
Y	X	W	V	W	V	W	V	U	V	Y
S	Y	X	W	S	T	V	W	X	Y	Z

Logidoku (page 116)

7	9	4	1	5	3	8	6	2
1	3	8	2	6	4	9	5	7
5	2	6	9	8	7	1	4	3
9	7	5	8	3	6	4	2	1
2	4	3	7	9	1	5	8	6
8	6	1	4	2	5	3	7	9
4	5	7	6	1	9	2	3	8
6	8	9	3	4	2	7	1	5
3	1	2	5	7	8	6	9	4

Star Power (page 117)

Geometric Shapes (page 117)

Answers

Sudoku (page 118)

3	5	1	4	2	7	8	6	9
7	2	8	1	9	6	4	5	3
6	4	9	5	3	8	1	7	2
1	3	5	8	4	2	6	9	7
2	7	6	9	5	1	3	4	8
8	9	4	6	7	3	5	2	1
9	1	7	3	6	5	2	8	4
5	8	2	7	1	4	9	3	6
4	6	3	2	8	9	7	1	5

Number Crossword (page 118)

5	5		
2	6	8	4
9	7	5	3
		8	5

Variety of V's (page 119)

1. vacuum cleaner; 2. valet; 3. vase; 4. venetian blinds; 5. vest; 6. view; 7. violets; 8. violin; 9. volcano; 10. volleyball

What Month's Next? (page 119)

The order is alphabetical so the next month is January.

Logidoku (page 121)

3	9	6	2	5	7	4	8	1
2	7	4	3	1	8	9	6	5
5	8	1	9	6	4	2	3	7
4	3	5	8	2	9	1	7	6
7	6	8	1	4	5	3	2	9
1	2	9	7	3	6	8	5	4
9	4	3	6	7	2	5	1	8
6	5	2	4	8	1	7	9	3
8	1	7	5	9	3	6	4	2

Fitting Words (page 121)

A	M	A	S	S
M	O	V	I	E
P	R	I	Z	E
S	E	D	E	R

Rhyme Time (page 122)

1. ray day; 2. blog log; 3. night bite; 4. steel heel; 5. trial smile; 6. grand brand; 7. found pound; 8. chrome home; 9. thrill hill; 10. attack back; 11. bring string; 12. prayer sayer; 13. turkey jerky; 14. sweeper keeper; 15. mention intention

A Lark in the Park (page 123)

In the bottom picture: 1. woman wearing heels; 2. baby in shopping cart; 3. blimp; 4. child has balloon in left hand; 5. statue holding broom; 6. kite has no tail; 7. skater wearing earmuffs; 8. cat in tree; 9. jogger has ponytail; 10. jogger wearing black shorts; 11. dog has no spots; 12. round streetlamp; 13. boy on bench doesn't have legs crossed; 14. man is reading *News*

Curvaceous Cube Construction (page 124)

Answer is B.

A Word to the Wise (page 125)

~~SE~~A~~V~~CO~~E~~M~~N~~M~~L~~O~~E~~N~~T~~WO~~TER~~RD~~S~~

The leftover letters spell "a common word."

Odd-Even Logidoku (page 125)

9	1	7	2	3	8	4	5	6
6	3	2	5	4	7	9	1	8
8	4	5	1	6	9	3	2	7
2	9	3	6	7	5	1	8	4
1	5	6	4	8	3	2	7	9
4	7	8	9	1	2	6	3	5
3	6	4	8	5	1	7	9	2
5	2	1	7	9	6	8	4	3
7	8	9	3	2	4	5	6	1

Ovoids Maze (page 126)

Fitting Words (page 127)

B	A	R	D	S
E	Q	U	I	P
A	U	G	E	R
N	A	S	T	Y

Geometric Shapes (page 127)

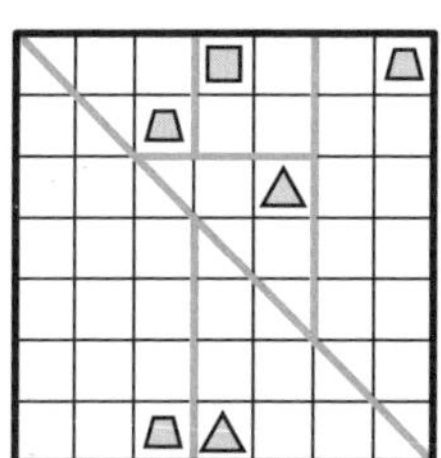

H. H. (pages 128–129)

```
Y H G R H S R                       H E H K H N H
A O N E A D U                       E S O C I O A
D M I T P L O                       D U U O T R L
I O T N H O H                       G O S H C D F
L H T U A H F                       E H E Y H E H
O A I H Z D L                       H T H L H H E
H B H D A N A                       O O O L I A A
H I D A R A H E H H C T I H F L A H G H L O K X R
G L R E D H E R H T H U L L H O U S E F D H E E T
I I A H A M H A N D E D S N R O H G N I T N U H E
H S H A R I A H E S R O H A Z E L H E N O M H E D
A E O R R D H A R D H A C K A H P E N N R U O A A
D Y B V D N U O H E R O H D E F O P R E R H P V E
D A B E D I H E S R O H M A E B N R O H P O H Y H
O H Y S D S E                       H H W H E H R
N N H T A A I                       S T A N A A E
H E O H D H G                       T A H D D N M
A L R O O A H                       R E E H D D M
L E S M A H H                       A H E M P E A
L H E E S H O                       H I H R E D H
```

Leftover letters spell: "Hertford, Hereford, and Hampshire," a reference to the song "The Rain in Spain" from the musical *My Fair Lady.*

Greedy Gears (page 130)

Sudoku (page 130)

8	3	5	4	7	2	6	1	9
1	7	2	3	9	6	5	8	4
4	6	9	8	1	5	3	2	7
7	2	6	1	5	4	8	9	3
5	8	1	2	3	9	4	7	6
3	9	4	6	8	7	1	5	2
2	5	8	9	6	3	7	4	1
9	1	3	7	4	8	2	6	5
6	4	7	5	2	1	9	3	8

Answers

Sketchbook (page 131)

Hexagonal Shift (page 132)

Get It? (page 132)

The long and the short of it

Bungled Burglary (page 133)

1. woman coming out of painting; 2. glass of water sitting on edge of window; 3. curtains don't match; 4. fish out of water; 5. thief has Santa hat; 6. thief has one bare foot; 7. dresser has zippers instead of knobs; 8. thief brought gifts; 9. bulldog has cat tail; 10. flowers have no stems into vase; 11. drawers hanging in mid-air; 12. Tiny's bowl is a hat; 13. screwdriver instead of knitting needle; 14. ball of yarn turns into a snake; 15. chair's arms turn into teddy bear feet; 16. slippers and socks attached to no one; 17. weeds growing in room

Temperature's Rising (pages 134–135)

E	L	I	S	■	I	P	A	S	S	■	L	A	C	E
L	E	N	O	■	D	A	R	T	H	■	E	B	A	N
C	O	L	D	T	U	R	K	E	Y	■	G	Y	R	O
I	N	E	A	R	N	E	S	T	■	M	I	S	T	S
D	A	T	S	U	N	■	■	■	L	A	S	S	O	■
■	■	■	■	C	O	O	L	M	I	L	L	I	O	N
A	N	I	S	E	■	N	O	I	R	■	A	N	N	A
L	I	N	T	■	M	A	G	M	A	■	T	I	E	R
A	C	T	A	■	I	L	I	E	■	R	E	A	D	Y
W	A	R	M	W	E	L	C	O	M	E	■	■	■	■
■	R	I	P	E	N	■	■	■	E	R	E	S	T	U
F	A	C	E	T	■	M	O	N	S	I	G	N	O	R
E	G	A	D	■	H	O	T	D	O	G	G	I	N	G
L	U	C	E	■	A	V	I	A	N	■	E	D	G	E
L	A	Y	S	■	D	E	S	K	S	■	D	E	A	D

The Times Are Changing! (page 136)

					20
2	4	5	3	2	240
1	3	3	5	5	225
2	3	1	4	4	96
3	2	5	4	1	120
1	3	4	2	2	48
12	216	300	480	80	48

Perfect Sunday Picnic? (page 136)

1. giant bird on bench; 2. soldiers on bird statue; 3. bat in daytime; 4. litter around trash basket; 5. snake in picnic basket; 6. man has 3 open cans; 7. cycler's feet not on pedals; 8. woman wearing 2 watches

Arrows (page 137)

	↘	↓	↘	↓	
→	1	4	3	5	↙
→	1	3	3	6	↖
→	1	3	4	4	↖
→	2	6	3	4	←
	↗	↑	↑	↑	

Sudoku (page 137)

5	7	1	8	9	3	4	2	6
9	2	8	4	5	6	7	1	3
3	6	4	2	7	1	8	5	9
2	3	5	1	6	8	9	7	4
4	8	9	7	2	5	6	3	1
6	1	7	9	3	4	5	8	2
1	9	3	6	8	7	2	4	5
7	5	2	3	4	9	1	6	8
8	4	6	5	1	2	3	9	7

A Beast of a Word Ladder! (page 138)

Answers may vary.

BEAST, least, leant, leans, loans, loins, joins, joint, point, paint, SAINT

Rhyme Time (page 139)

1. sly buy; 2. cub grub; 3. Mister Lister; 4. dues news; 5. over Dover; 6. bake snake; 7. most toast; 8. come scrum; 9. sharp carp; 10. wheel deal; 11. smart start; 12. witch pitch; 13. seize cheese; 14. relate great; 15. puerile mural; 16. foremost host; 17. durable thurible; 18. indentation examination; 19. introspective detective; 20. controversial commercial

How to Turn a Lemon into an Apple (page 140)

LEMON: Change M to A to get LEAON, an anagram of ALONE.

Change O to P to get ALPNE, an anagram of PLANE.

Change N to P to get PLAPE, an anagram of APPLE.

Word Jigsaw (page 140)

Milky Way (page 141)

Geometric Shapes (page 141)

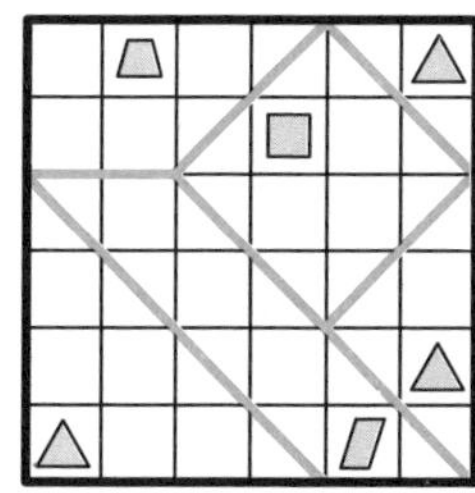

Four Magic Words (page 142)

			F	O	R			P	H	I
C	O	S	I	N	E		L	O	A	N
I	N	A	R	O	W		O	O	P	S
R	A	M	S		A	D	O	L	P	H
C	L	O	T		R	U	S	H	E	R
A	L	A	M	O	D	E		A	N	E
			A	D	S		S	L	E	D
B	O	L	T	S	■	W	I	L	D	S
A	L	E	E		S	O	D			
D	I	G		S	T	E	E	R	E	D
A	V	A	T	A	R		O	H	N	O
P	E	T	U	L	A		R	O	T	O
P	O	E	T		N	O	D	D	E	D
L	I	E	U		D	R	E	A	R	Y
E	L	S			S	S	R			

Look at that Charter Cutie! (page 143)

The anagrammed words: TRITE CHAUCER (ARCHITECTURE); CARGO HITCH (GOTHIC ARCH); COSTLIER (CLOISTER); CHARIOT INN (CORINTHIAN); STEEL PAD (PEDESTAL); LASER TIP (PILASTER); BUST REST (BUTTRESS); ROYAL EGG (GARGOYLE).

Answers

Presidential Portraits (pages 144–145)

B	L	A	H	■	B	I	R	D	■	H	B	O	M	B
I	O	N	A	■	E	R	I	E	■	A	R	N	I	E
T	O	N	I	■	N	O	N	E	■	T	I	T	L	E
S	T	A	R	T	I	N	G	P	I	T	C	H	E	R
■	■	■	D	O	G	S	■	■	P	E	K	E	■	■
D	A	C	R	O	N	■	T	S	A	R	■	M	O	D
E	T	A	I	L	■	S	I	N	S	■	H	O	L	A
L	E	S	E	■	A	P	L	U	S	■	U	N	I	T
L	A	H	R	■	G	R	E	G	■	A	L	E	V	E
A	R	A	■	W	A	Y	S	■	P	L	A	Y	E	D
■	■	S	T	O	P	■	■	S	E	E	S	■	■	■
F	I	S	H	N	E	T	S	T	O	C	K	I	N	G
A	V	E	R	T	■	A	P	O	P	■	I	T	E	M
M	E	T	O	O	■	R	A	U	L	■	R	O	M	E
E	S	S	E	N	■	A	N	T	E	■	T	R	O	N

Quorum of Q's (page 146)

1. quadrilateral, 2. quadrant, 3. quail, 4. quill, 5. quilt, 6. quiver

Supply Yourself! (page 147)

113

No Business Like Snow Business (page 147)

The women are the better workers: 3 women can shovel as much snow as 5 men.

An algebraic equation is: $10(8M + 12W) = 12(10M + 8W)$. Solving: $24W = 40M$, which simplifies to $3W = 5M$

Three Stories (page 149)

ED appears 50 times, DEE appears 36 times, and DEEDEE appears 8 times. Each of them can hold a DEED.

Eat Your Words (pages 150–151)

Cross-Country Maze (page 152)

Waste Not, Want Not (page 153)

Answers may vary.
HOARD, board, boars, soars, scars, scans, scant, scent, spent, SPEND

Card Trick (page 154)

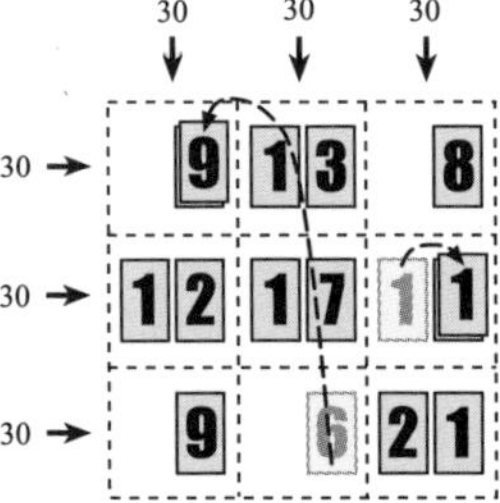

Tamagram (page 154)

MILK FRAME (FILMMAKER).

Crypto-Botany (page 155)

Bleeding Hearts (name of plant)
Bleeding Hearts are old-fashioned sentimental favorites. They have unique heart-shaped flowers with teardrop-shaped, protruding petals, which makes them look as if they are bleeding.

Frequent Flier (pages 156–157)

A Startling Word Puzzle (page 158)

Just as we said, the answer is STARTLING! The 8 other words you formed from it may vary.
STARTLING – L = STARTING
STARTING – T = STARING
STARING – A = STRING
STRING – R = STING
STING – T = SING
SING – G = SIN
SIN – S = IN
IN – N = I

Word Jigsaw (page 159)

Geometric Shapes (page 159)

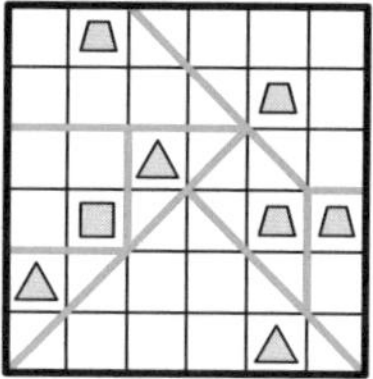

Loop the Loops Maze (page 160)

Add It Up (page 161)

										63
7	5	8	3	2	2	6	5	1	8	47
1	2	5	3	2	1	6	5	8	9	42
7	3	4	2	1	6	5	8	1	2	39
1	6	2	3	8	1	7	4	9	5	46
9	1	4	3	1	5	1	2	3	9	38
5	5	9	1	6	5	4	6	5	7	53
8	8	6	9	4	6	2	8	9	2	62
6	2	1	3	7	4	7	7	1	8	46
7	7	2	5	3	8	3	2	3	7	47
4	3	8	4	2	4	1	4	5	9	44
55	42	49	36	36	42	42	51	45	66	43

The Missing Numbers (page 161)

A. 8; B. 6, 7; C. 16; D. 12; E. 14

Answers

Concert in the Park (page 162)

1. paper boat on top of gazebo; 2. shingles different on gazebo; 3. "today" spelled wrong; 4. balloon floating upside down; 5. giant watch in balloons; 6. rocket instead of microphone for singer; 7. conductor has 3 arms; 8. portion of gazebo leg missing; 9. eskimos holding balloons; 10. dog leash has ladle attached; 11. seal balancing ball; 12. umbrella upside down; 13. park bench blocking sidewalk; 14. man on bench has foot in pot; 15. woman has scuba fin on; 16. man's chair is a racing flag; 17. man using bottles as binoculars; 18. man's glasses upside down; 19. whisk broom for head; 20. dog dish for hat; 21. man's ear missing; 22. woman's bun is a baseball

Cube Conundrum (page 163)

3 and 5 are impossible

Grid Computing (page 165)

A 6	B 3	C 7
D 1	E 5	F 4
G 9	H 2	J 8

Alphabet Jigsaw (page 165)

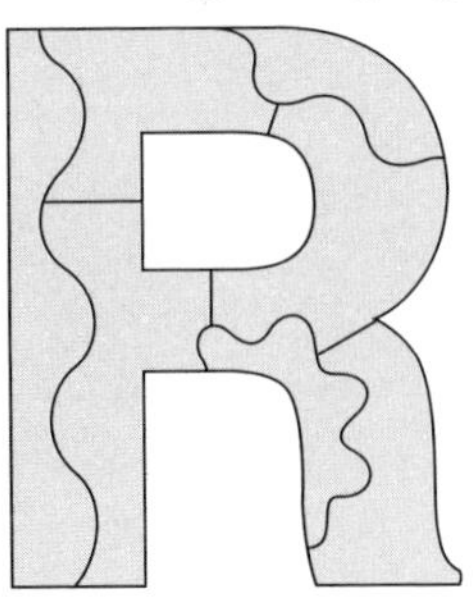

Head Turners (page 166)

```
        E V L L E R B
      Y R I W F O O D Y
  N A Y V E L A J O N E N X
  P I E R O V E R O T O R E
S S T P G E M O T D E B P I O
N S W I C S I G N M L L E E N W H
I I C L E T T A N T E T O P L E H
N T U E P T M H S I S R O T C T H
E B L A R A O R E A S O S N S L O
S N R A R O I N S B H R E P O P G
E T G C N F S I B S O F A O O N N
I N G I E A D L K O R T P P I T W
  O R H S E C I O A O H T R D I
    T S S S R S I S A K M L P
    E L L T T L U L E O E D E
        B A C O L E O R K
          W A R P D Z D
```

Theme: One word in each of the phrases is spelled backward.

Tamagram (page 167)

TABLE MAKER (MARKETABLE)

Triangle Trial (page 167)

There are 35 triangles:
△ABC; △ABD; △ABE; △ABF; △ABG; △ABH; △ACD; △ACE; △ADE; △AEF; △AEG; △AFG; △AEJ; △ADH; △ACJ; △BCD; △BCE; △BCG; △BCH; △BCI; △BDE; △BDF; △BEI; △BGH; △CDE; △CDH; △CDI; △CDJ; △CEG; △CHI; △DEF; △DEI; △DEJ; △DIJ; △EFJ

Island Survivors (page 168)

1. picture is flopped; 2. no sun; 3. monkey has no coconut; 4. palm frond missing behind monkey; 5. different markings on palm tree; 6. 2 coconuts in tree; 7. man waving stick instead of flag; 8. different flag; 9. flag man wearing hat; 10. flag man has vest; 11. flag man has long pants; 12. only 2 birds in sky; 13. ship has 2 smoke stacks; 14. little cloud missing; 15. bird attacking man; 16. man's mouth closed; 17. man missing stripe on shirt; 18. man has ragged pants; 19. different plants; 20. woman has short hair; 21. woman has short sleeves; 22. woman has black pants; 23. woman wearing shoes; 24. different fish on line: 25. outboard motor instead of oars; 26. no water barrel; 27. fishing poles; 28. bag has black handles; 29. suitcase has different stickers; 30. bananas on spit; 31. starfish and shell reversed positions.

INDEX

continued on page 192

Index